THE ISLAMIC PERSPECTIVE

An Aspect of British Architecture and Design

in the 19th century

MICHAEL DARBY

In Memory
of
Melissa
Prewatt

Leighton House Gallery

The Royal Borough of Kensington and Chelsea, London.

A WORLD OF ISLAM FESTIVAL TRUST PUBLICATION

The Islamic Perspective
Designed and produced for
The World of Islam Festival Trust
by Scorpion Pica Ltd
Distributed by Scorpion Communications
377 High Street, Stratford, London E15 4QZ

© Michael Darby 1983
First published 1983
ISBN 0 905035 31 3

Designer: Colin Larkin
Mechanicals: Dale Dawson
Editor: Leonard Harrow
Co-ordinator: Alistair Duncan
Phototypeset in 10 on 11 Melior
by Scorpion Pica
400A Hale End Road, London E4 9PB
printed on 115gsm matt art, by
Hazell Watson and Viney, England

Photographic credits
Tony Bentley fig. 3
Norman Brand 85
British Architectural Library 1, 24, 25, 52, 66, 67, 110, 113, fig. 4
British Library 5
Country Life 10, 114
Courtauld Institute of Art: Photographic Survey 4, 8, 15, 47, 78,
    80
Greater London Council 56, 71
Guildhall Art Gallery and Museum 69
Hastings Museum and Art Gallery 115
A.F. Kersting 111
National Monuments Record 50, 51, 95, 116
Reilly and Constantine Commercial 68
Royal Borough of Kensington and Chelsea Public Libraries 53, 55
Victoria and Albert Museum 46, 48, 49, 69, 75, 86, 88, 91, 93, 94,
    98, 99, 106

Michael Darby was born in 1944. He was educated at Rugby School and subsequently at Reading University where he completed a Ph.D. in 1974 on the work of Owen Jones. He joined the staff of the Victoria and Albert Museum in 1964 and worked firstly in the Department of Textiles and later in the Department of Prints and Drawings. In 1976 he was promoted to take charge of the Museum's temporary exhibition programme. He has written many articles on various aspects of architecture and the decorative arts, and was co-author with John Physick of the catalogue of the 'Marble Halls' exhibition in 1973. His most recent publications are a book about British Art in the Museum and a catalogue of the drawings of the Victorian architect John Pollard Seddon. He is married, and in his spare time is an enthusiastic amateur entomologist.

CONTENTS

LIST OF FIGURES

LIST OF LENDERS

FOREWORD BY HIS ROYAL HIGHNESS THE DUKE OF GLOUCESTER, G.C.V.O.

Some great works of architecture are created through the skill of individuals, whose genius enables them to master not only the great mass of a building but also the details that tie all the varied parts together. But most of the buildings that are universally admired are those which are the consequence of a tradition in which many anonymous craftsmen and builders have worked over a great period of time – possibly centuries – to refine a style and a vocabulary of details that can be applied to many types of building.

The Islamic style is of the latter kind of creativity in which the decorative detailing flows from the structural system of the building, and the quality of the craftsmanship demonstrates that nothing should be spared to achieve perfection.

This exhibition shows how this Islamic tradition was first reported, and then slowly revealed to the British public by writers, artists and finally architects, as the interest of the public was increasingly diverted from Europe – hitherto the sole source of imported architectural styles – to more eastern countries as commerce and politics brought greater interdependence.

This knowledge coincided with the expansive confidence of the Victorian Era, when our classical tradition seemed too restrictive for a country with world-wide interests and ambitions.

This exhibition reveals which aspects of the Islamic tradition were most admired and found most suitable for incorporation in the new eclectic school of building.

I hope that many people will enjoy seeing an exhibition, which demonstrates so clearly the influence that one great culture can have on another given favourable circumstances for cohesion.

PREFACE

This exhibition sets out to document an aspect of mid 19th century British architecture and design – the influence of Islamic buildings and their decoration – which has been largely ignored by modern historians. The abstract, experimental and conceptual concerns engendered by the Islamic experience have proved difficult to interpret, and much of what was built has now been altered or demolished. In accepting the existence of an Islamic 'revival', in the sense of the Gothic and Classical revivals on which so much 19th century architectural history has concentrated, however, a framework is provided within which the work of a number of architects and artists, who are at present little known, becomes intelligible. Foremost among them is undoubtedly Owen Jones, one of the most important but least studied theorists of the last century, and a large part of the exhibition is devoted to him as a result. In so far as Islamic influence played a part in the development of colour printing, the acceptance of architectural polychromy, the introduction of new building materials, the teaching of art and the appearance of textiles, wallpapers, books and other decorative arts, it could also be said that this framework permits new light to be shed on many of the fundamental problems which confronted architecture and design in the middle of the last century.

Numerous previous exhibitions have covered the work of painters in the Near East, and I have deliberately set out to exclude them in consequence. Those who are included were either trained as architects or their work assists the better understanding of the other drawings exhibited. Some critics will say, no doubt, that I should have included at least one drawing by David Roberts, but his work, like that of John Frederick Lewis, is already well known and stands outside the central theme of this exhibition, albeit marginally.

A word is necessary, perhaps, about my interpretation of the term Islamic. I have taken this to cover architecture throughout the area embraced by Muslim conquests, from the great Umayyad and Nasrid dynasties which ruled much of Spain in the west, to the Mughal emperors of India in the east. I am not an Islamic historian and have visited few of the buildings mentioned outside Great Britain. I hope that I may be forgiven, therefore, for the obvious failings of this account in that respect.

ACKNOWLEDGEMENTS

My first expression of thanks must be to His Royal Highness the Duke of Gloucester who, in spite of many important commitments, very kindly agreed to write the Foreword to this catalogue.

I owe thanks to many people who have helped me to prepare this exhibition, but would like to express a special debt of gratitude to Rodney Searight who has not only been very generous in allowing me to borrow from his magnificent collection and in giving me the benefit of his vast knowledge, but whose own enthusiasm for the subject was a constant source of encouragement. I must also mention particularly Mrs A.F.C. de Cosson, who very kindly allowed me to go through the material relating to Joseph Bonomi in her possession, and who has allowed me to borrow the diary of his visit to the Holy Land; and the Reverend Selwyn Tillett who most unselfishly lent me his manuscript biography of Robert Hay – a fund of information incorporating some of the meticulous research he has carried out over several years. It is very much to be hoped that this important book will be published shortly.

My colleagues in the Victoria and Albert Museum have, as always, been supportive, and I am very grateful to them, particularly since my activities in this instance have been 'extra curricular' so to speak. I must mention especially Sir Roy Strong and John Physick who allowed me to take it on; Shirley Bury, Michael Kauffmann, Santina Levey, Ronald Lightbown, Anthony Radcliffe, Robert Skelton, and Peter Thornton, the Keepers who have permitted me to borrow from their Departments; Julian Litten, Anne Buddle and the paperkeepers in Prints and Drawings, who have had to open cupboards endlessly, and who prepared their drawings for exhibition; Michael Snodin who took the time to look out some early drawings which were unknown to me; Duncan Haldane who talked over the loans from the National Art Library; Sue Stronge, who scoured the Indian collections for objects purchased from the Great Exhibition; Clive Wainwright who helped to locate information in the archives of the Furniture and Woodwork Department; Natalie Rothstein who helped me in the Textile Department; Simon Tait, the Museum's Press Officer, who has advised us on publicity matters; and lastly my assistant Garth Hall who has, as always, given me great support.

Outside the Museum I must thank John Harris, Margaret Richardson, Jane Preger, Nicholas Antram and Robert Elwall at the British Architectural Library, who helped me with material from their collection, and Lynne Hutton, their Press Officer who supplied me with a list; Peter Howell for bringing various 'Alhambresque' objects to my notice, including the plaster panel which he has kindly lent; Jessica Rutherford and Patrick Conner at Brighton, who allowed me to borrow the engraving of Porden's stables; Mr Curle at Kensington Reference Library, who looked out material and kindly framed his loans for me; Pauline Rohatgi at the India Office Library and Records, who helped with the loan of the rare print by William Hodges; David Watkin for supplying the photograph of Cockerell's drawing; Victoria Williams for arranging photography at Hastings Museum; Stephen Croad and his colleagues at the National Monuments Record, who supplied photographs from their collection; and Briony Llewellyn who generously offered as much help as I needed.

Finally I must express a special debt of gratitude to the Trustees of the World of Islam Festival Trust who have sponsored the exhibition, and to the Trust's director Alistair Duncan and his assistant Eleanor Cozens without both of whose constant support, guidance and very hard work the exhibition could never have taken place; my wife whose work on 19th century sculpture continues to throw up an endless supply of useful references for me, and who solved several problems; Sally Chappell who undertook most of the photogaphy for the catalogue; and lastly Leonard Harrow and Colin Larkin of Scorpion Pica for editing the catalogue so skilfully, and for seeing it through the press.

NOTE ON SPELLING

There are several erudite systems for transliterating words out of non-Roman scripts and although purists might like to see such spellings with their diacritical marks within these pages, the spelling of foreign words has generally been left as they originally appeared in English. This will hopefully avoid confusion, especially as many unscientific spellings have gained their own currency in modern English.

SECTION 1

PROLOGUE

This section includes eleven objects dating from the middle of the 18th century which have been selected, as the title suggests, to give an indication of the attitudes to Islamic architecture and decoration prevailing before the work of the architects and draughtsmen of the early 19th century. It should not be thought, however, that interest in the Near East and its influence on British buildings commenced in 1750, in fact, it began long before that.

Occasional traders, pilgrims and other travellers visited the Near East at the time of Marco Polo and before, but the inception of firm ties with the countries of the eastern Mediterranean waited until 1581 when the Levant Company was granted its charter by Queen Elizabeth I. The 'Turkey merchants', as the members of the Company were called, installed agents in Constantinople, Aleppo and elsewhere, and available evidence points to a considerable trade, particularly in textiles, by the end of the 17th century. Perhaps the most noticeable consequence in England of this contact with the Islamic world was the setting up of Turkish baths and coffee houses from the 17th century. One of the first Turkish baths in London opened off Newgate Street in 1679, and was described by John Strype when revising Stowe's *Survey of London* (1720), as a 'neat contrived building after the Turkish mode for that purpose ... much resorted into for Sweating, being found very good for aches etc.'[1] The 'Turkish mode' involved rooms lined with Dutch tiles, and a cupola over the main hall. Other baths existed in Chancery Lane and Long Acre, and Turks themselves were even brought to England to practise their 'champooing' and massage skills.

The first coffee house was also opened in the 17th century, by Edward Daniels, a merchant from Smyrna, who installed his servant Pasquee Rosee as the proprietor. Coffee drinking quickly became popular, and other houses followed, including the famous 'Sultaness Head' which opened in Cornhill in 1658. Supplies of beans were imported by the East India Company from Mokha in the Yemen, and by the Levant Company from Aleppo.[2] The introduction of names for such establishments which denoted their Levantine origin was common. The 'Sultan's Head' coffee house, for example,

opened in Aldersgate Street in 1698, and Bryant Lillywhite records the existence of more than one hundred 'Turk's Head' inns, coffee houses, etc. before 1850, of which the majority were opened in the 17th and 18th centuries.[3]

While the activities of the Levant and East India Companies brought direct contact with the Near East for a small number, the publications of travellers were the only source of information for the vast majority of the British public. Books in English about the Near East may be said to have begun with Richard Hakluyt's *Principal Navigations*, first published in 1598, and to have continued in ever increasing numbers since. Many of these volumes mention Islamic buildings. The Reverend John Cartwright, in his *Preacher's Travels* (1611), for example, described the royal palace in Isfahan shortly after it had been completed: 'the walls glister with red Marbel, and pargeting of divers colours; yea, all the Palace is paved with Checker and Tesseled worke ... the windows of Alabaster, white Marbel and much other spotted Marbel'; and Henry Teonge, whose diary of travels in the Levant in the 1670s was edited and published by Charles Knight in 1825, wrote of Aleppo: 'next you see the coopelows, which are in abundance not only on their moskeus, but on many of their great buildings, rising up over the rest of the buildings like so many pretty mountains over the plains'. Perhaps it was descriptions such as these which prompted Sir Christopher Wren to correspond in 1670 with Dudley North, the treasurer of the Levant Company in Constantinople, about the structure of the roofs of S. Sofia, and which caused him to alter his designs for the interior of St. Paul's to include saucer shaped vaults, as a result.[4]

Of volumes published in the first half of the 18th century Richard Pococke's *Description of the East* (1743) is perhaps the most impressive, and includes plans and elevations of various buildings amongst which is the 'Mosque of Solomon's Temple' in Damascus. Like the Reverend Aaron Hill's *A Full and Just Account of the Present State of the Ottoman Empire* (1709), written after 'a serious observation taken in many years travels through those countries', which includes a 'prospect' and 'inward plan' of the 'Grand Signiors'' palace and seraglio at

9

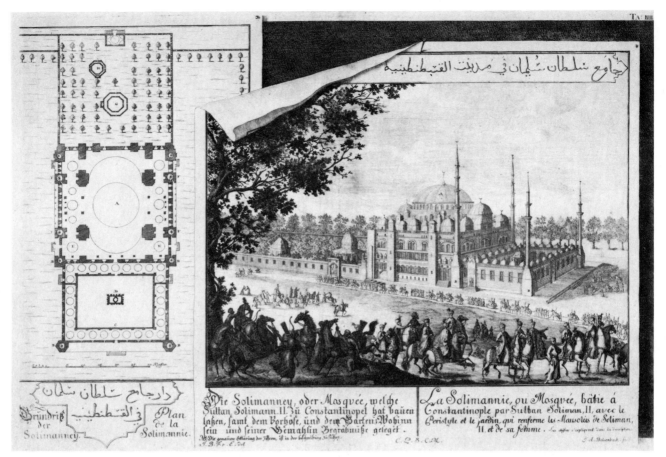

Figure 1

Constantinople, Pococke's drawings are idealized rather than accurate studies. There is, however, a sense of a genuine wish not only to understand more about Islamic methods of construction, but also more about the history of Islamic architecture by the middle of the century. Pococke did considerable research for his book, and describes in detail, not simply churches, palaces and mosques, but also hospitals and other more menial buildings. Thomas Shaw, *Travels or Observations relating to several parts of Barbary and the Levant* (1757), includes a whole section entitled 'Of their architecture and method of building', but does so in the realisation that contemporary methods of construction and use may throw more light on '*those* that are occasionally mentioned in the H. Scriptures', and that 'a particular account may not a little clear up such doubts and difficulties as have arisen '.

Complementary with the escalating numbers of books about the Near East which were published in the 18th century, was an increase in the proportion of Grand Tourists who extended their travels to include areas east of Greece. Lord Sandwich visited Constantinople, Asia Minor and Egypt in 1738, and Charles Perry travelled to the same places shortly after. William Ponsonby explored Asia Minor, and Frederick Battimore visited Turkey in 1763.

'Twas all whimsical and charming' wrote Lady Mary Wortley when in 1716 she heard of her husband's appointment as Ambassador Extraordinary to the Court of Turkey.[5] Her reaction

appears to epitomise the contemporary view of the Near East, as revealed in publications like the *Arabian Nights Entertainments* or *The Thousand and One Nights*, which was made known in Europe early in the 18th century by the translation into French of Antoine Galland. Similarly, the interest of British architects in Islamic buildings tended to concentrate on their picturesque qualities. Thus, although the church of S. Sophia continued to be a source for serious works (James Wyatt using it as a prototype for the Pantheon in 1770[6]), for the most part the influence of this and other Near Eastern buildings was felt in garden architecture, where 'Mosques' and 'Turkish tents' readily joined the repertoire of exotic structures suitable for adorning country house parks.[7]

The main source of information for the architects like William Chambers, Henry Keene and Johann Müntz, who designed these garden buildings, was Johann B. Fischer von Erlach's *Entwurff einer historischen Architectur* (1725), which was translated into English in 1730 and 1737 (fig. 1). But von Erlach's drawings, like those of Pococke and Perry are simplified, and as William Wrighte, who included several designs for 'Mosques' in his *Grotesque Architecture or Rural Amusement* (1767) reveals, real knowledge about Islamic buildings at this time was still very slight: 'the minarets are placed in the Plan by way of ornament to shew the true Taste of the Turkish buildings; and the Singularity of the Stile of Architecture is such that

10

Figure 2

will render it a very pleasing Ornament, if executed in a Pleasure Ground, or upon an elevated verdant Amphitheatre. It may be built of Wood, and stucco'd; the inside should be painted with various rich colours, which would have a pleasing and elegant appearance ... the Minarets should be solid, and the Pedestals ... should be decorated with Arabic inscriptions.' He also explained that 'in the Spandrells are Moors Heads, with Crescents, Roses and Stars ... the Stile of Architecture is a Medium between the Chinese and Gothic having neither the Levity of the former nor the Gravity of the latter.'

Eighteenth century picturesque and romantic taste also welcomed the incursion of exoticism into many other areas, and numerous examples may be cited, from the 'Divan Club', of which Sir Francis Dashwood and his wife were members with Lady Mary Wortley Montagu,[8] to the furnishing of interiors and the design of household objects. William Beckford, the author of *Vathek* (1782), subtitled in later editions 'An Arabian Tale', commissioned metalwork from Thomas Angell with Islamic designs; had a coffer made 'in the Persian Taste'; and installed a bedroom at Fonthill 'most elegant ... fitted up in the Turkish stile'.[9]

The boundaries of the Islamic empire extended, of course, far beyond Turkey to embrace both India in the east, and Spain in the west, and it was to these areas that the attention of travellers and others turned in the closing decades of the 18th century. The results of the work of British artists in India after 1760 was surveyed in the *India Observed* exhibition at the Victoria and Albert Museum last year. Of the many prints, drawings and paintings displayed, those by William Hodges, and Thomas and William Daniell undoubtedly had the greatest impact on British architecture. William Hodges, the author of *Select Views in India* (1785-88), was a close neighbour of George Dance, and it is thought that the 'Indian' turrets which appear in his designs probably resulted from Hodges's influence. The design of Sezincote (no. 10), on the other hand, certainly resulted from the influence of the Daniell's *Oriental Scenery* (1795-1805), as did many of the early designs for the Royal Pavilion at Brighton (no. 9, fig. 2).[10]

In the work of Hodges and the Daniells is to be discerned evidence of the more serious approach to Islamic buildings which characterises the work of the architects and topographical artists of the 1830s and later. Sir William Jones, the founder of the Asiatic Society of Bengal, itself a pioneering venture, emphasised the 'correctness' of Hodges's *Views* in an address to the members, and Hodges himself published a *Dissertation on the Prototypes of Architecture, Hindoo, Moorish and Gothic* (1787) (no. 5) in which he pointed out the irrationality of contemporary admiration for classical buildings at the expense of all others.

While Hodges and the Daniells interested themselves in Indian buildings, the Irish architect James Cavanah Murphy was visiting Portugal in order to make the ground plans and elevations of the great monastery at Batalha which he published in 1795. The inspiration for the design of this building, and many others in Portugal erected during the reign of Manoel I (1495-1521), is unclear, but includes an undeniably Islamic element. This does not appear to derive so much from the work of the great Umayyad and Nasrid dynasties which had dominated the Iberian peninsular for many centuries previously, as from eastern sources introduced to Portugal following Vasco da Gama's opening of the sea route to India, and the rapid expansion of trade which resulted. The success of Murphy's first volume induced him to return to Spain in 1802 for a further seven years to make the drawings for a second volume entitled *The Arabian Antiquities of Spain* which was published in 1815. (no. 7)

Many travellers to Spain before Murphy had published accounts of their journeys which reproduced drawings of architecture. Henry Swinburne, for example, whose *Travels through Spain in the years 1775 and 1776* (1779), included plans, elevations and details of the Alhambra; William Jacob, who introduced a double page elevation of the Palace of Charles V in Granada, in his *Travels in the South of Spain in Letters written AD 1809 and 1810* (1811); and Sir John Carr who also included a view of the Alhambra in his *Descriptive Travels in the Southern and Eastern Parts of Spain and the Balearic Isles in the year 1809* (1811). When compared with the illustrations of Murphy, however, these studies appear very slight. But, although one may feel inclined to place Murphy in the second section of this exhibition on the basis of the *Arabian Antiquities*, he appears here, not simply because his work was so inaccurate, but also because his interest appears to have stemmed from antiquarian and archaeological studies rather than from a desire to understand the nature of the Islamic experience which motivated the architects who followed him.

Notes

1 Quoted by Sarah Searight, *The British in the Middle East*, 1969, p. 21.
2 On early coffee houses see Bryant Lillywhite, *London Coffee Houses*, 1963.
3 Bryant Lillywhite, *London Signs*, 1972.
4 Kerry Downes, *Christopher Wren*, 1971, p. 163.
5 Quoted by Sarah Searight, op. cit..
6 John Summerson, *Architecture in Britain 1530-1830*, 1970, pp. 458, 556. He also notes that plans of S. Sophia exist among the papers of Robert Adam in the Royal Institute of British Architects.
7 Patrick Conner, *Oriental Architecture in the West*, 1979, lists various examples.
8 There are portraits of them in Turkish dress at West Wycombe Park.
9 A cup and cover by Angell is in the Victoria and Albert Museum (428-1882). This was exhibited in the William Beckford exhibition, 1976 (C. 15), the catalogue of which mentions the coffer and Turkish room (p. 79).
10 P. Conner, op. cit., mentions these and other 'Indian' designs.

MÜNTZ, Johann Henry (1727-1798)

1 Design for the Alhambra, Kew Gardens. 1750.
A plan associated with this elevation is inscribed by Sir William Chambers *Plan & Elevation of a building in the old Moorish Taste* and by Müntz *this I drew in 1750 for the Prince & model was made of it and it was built in 1758.*
Pen and ink, water-colour and gold paint. 36.4 × 32.6
British Architectural Library: Drawings Collection

It was thought at first that this drawing represented an early design by Chambers for the Alhambra at Kew Gardens, one of a number of exotic buildings which he designed for Frederick, Prince of Wales and his wife Augusta. Harris has suggested, however, that the drawing is by Müntz on the basis of the similarity of the draughtsmanship to that in Müntz, 'Proposals for Publishing ... A Course of Gothic Architecture' (1760), and because in this work Müntz promises to publish 'a Temple for a garden in the Moresque stile, of the Author's Composition, and which is going to be executed at a Nobleman's Seat'.

Müntz is known to have provided the designs for the Gothic Cathedral at Kew which Chambers built, and it is assumed that this drawing represents an early design which Chambers altered in execution by the addition of Gothic and Classical features. Müntz, who was born at Mulhausen, is known to have visited Spain before he arrived in England as the protégé of Horace Walpole. He mentions in the 'Proposals' that in 1748 he drew 'some remarkable fine and curious Remains of Moresque Fabrics, still existing in the kingdoms of Murcia, Valentia, and the City of Saragossa in Spain', and he could have done sketches there on which he based this design. Indeed, the possibilty arises that this drawing may have been done at that time and that it represents a building which Müntz saw, but the design is so unlike any Moorish buildings of which the author is aware, that this seems unlikely. Harris suggests that Chambers met Müntz in Paris in 1750 and that is presumably when the design was prepared.

This drawing was originally in the collection of John, 3rd Earl of Bute, who was adviser to the Princess of Wales at Kew.

The Alhambra has now been demolished.

Lit. J. Harris, 'Exoticism at Kew', *Apollo*, August 1963, pp. 103-8.
J. Harris, *Sir William Chambers*, 1970, pp. 37, 38, pls. 24, 25.
Catalogue of the Drawings Collection of the Royal Institute of British Architects, L-N, 1973.

KEENE, Henry (1726-1776)

2 Plan and elevation of a 'Mosque'. 1759-63.
Pen and ink, and wash. 28.6 × 48.2.
Victoria and Albert Museum (E. 890-1921)

This design is apparently based on the mosque at Kew Gardens which Sir William Chambers built for the Prince and Princess of Wales in about 1758. Chambers, who noted that the Kew mosque incorporated the 'Principal peculiarities of the Turkish Architecture', adapted his design in turn from J.B. Fischer von Erlach, *Entwurff einer historischen Architectur* (1725), which was translated and published in England in 1730 and 1737. The third 'book' of Fischer's work 'Containing Fifteen Plates describing The Buildings of the Arabians, Turks, etc. together with some modern One's of the Persians, Siamese, Chinese & Japonese', was, perhaps, more influential than any other publication in providing the inspiration for exotic garden buildings in the 18th century. Chambers apparently based his mosque on 'the Imperial Bath, near the City of Buda in Hungary, remarkable as well on Account of the Virtue of its Waters, as the Excellence of the Arabian Architecture', and on the 'great and stately Moskee, built by the Sultan Achment at Constantinople in the Year 1610'. Inside, the walls were painted by Richard Wilson, not with coloured geometrical patterns, but with curtains draped from palm trees.

It is worth noting that Chambers' mosque at Kew was probably also the inspiration for the 'Rural Mosque with Minarets', the 'Circular Mosque with Cabinets attached', and the 'Turkish Mosque with Minarets attached' which are illustrated in William Wrighte, *Grotesque Architecture or Rural Amusement* (1767).

Henry Keene rebuilt the east front of Hartwell House for Sir William Lee, Bart., between 1759 and 1763 and is known to have carried out other works in the park including a bridge and a mosque. It is possible, therefore, that this design may have been intended for Hartwell.

Lit. J. Harris, *Sir William Chambers*, 1970, p. 37.

KEENE, Henry (1726-1776)

3 Design for a tent. c.1765
Pen and ink, and water-colour. 29.5 × 19
Victoria and Albert Museum (E. 916-1921)

'Turkish tents' like 'mosques' were one of the more popular manifestations of the exotic taste of the 18th century. No doubt conceived as attractive means of providing temporary shelter in gardens, most, like this splendid example designed for an unknown patron, survive only as drawings. The first recorded Turkish tent appears to be that erected at Stourhead some time after 1754, at the eastern end of the lake, which was painted inside with a blue and white mosaic pattern. Conner notices other 18th century examples at Painshill, Vauxhall, Bellevue in Ireland, and Boughton; and an early 19th century example at Virginia Water in which George IV dined shortly before his death. The tent at Boughton, which was more Chinese, perhaps, than Turkish, may have been that which formerly stood in the grounds of Montagu House, Whitehall; while that at Painshill was sketched by the Swede Frederick Piper, who was so taken with it that he erected two similar examples in Sweden after his return in 1780. One of these is the extraordinary *Corps de garde* in Drottningholm Park, which is made of metal.

The Stourhead tent was removed by Sir Richard Colt Hoare in the 1790s in response to changes in fashion. The seriousness of the neo-Classical period saw little merit in the frivolities of the mid-century.

1

Other tents no doubt disappeared in this way too, but the majority must surely have perished through being exposed to the weather or through being constantly taken down and folded up. Like so many of the magnificent tents so popular in Mughal India, some of which were brought back to this country by the Raj, most have also disappeared. Tipoo's tent, now at Powys, which was used by Lord Clive and was shown last year in the Victoria and Albert Museum's *Indian Heritage* exhibition, is a very rare survival.

Lit. P. Conner, *op. cit.*, 1979, pp. 73-75.

BORRA, Giovanni Batista (1712-1786)

4 View of the Mosque of S. Sophia, Istanbul. c.1750.
Pen and ink, and water-colour. 56.8 × 40.3.
Searight Collection.

There were two Italian architects of this name. The Borra who executed this view appears to have been born in Turin and to have carried out various works in England, including buildings at Stowe between 1751 and 1764 for Lord Temple, and the music room, now in the Victoria and Albert Museum, for the Duke of Norfolk's house in St. James's Square.

2

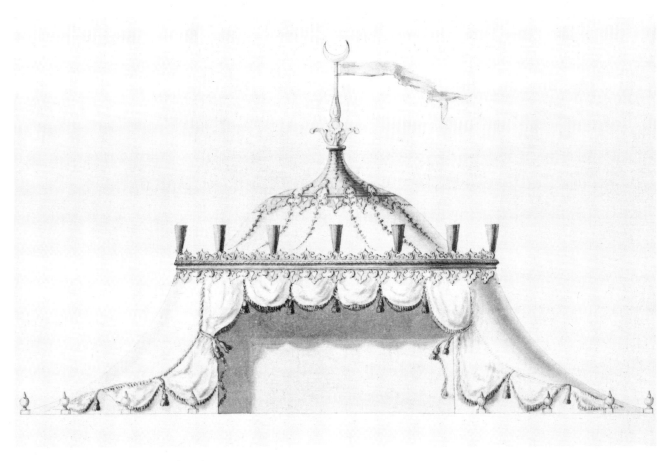

3

4

5

Shortly before coming to England Borra accompanied James Dawkins and Robert Wood on their journey to Palmyra and carried out the illustrations for their *The Ruins of Palmyra, otherwise Tedmor in the Desert* (1753), the original drawings for which are now in the British Architectural Library, Drawings Collection, the Mellon Collection and the Society for the Promotion of Hellenic Studies.

This and other views of Istanbul in the Searight Collection, although worked up by Borra in England from smaller sketches done on the spot, are much less accurate than his drawings of Palmyra. His visit to Turkey must have been his first experience of Islamic and Byzantine architecture, and he apparently found it difficult not to give the buildings a rather classical aspect: thus the curious finial on top of the dome and the strange appearance of the building to the right of the Mosque. Likewise the scale and detail of the gate of the seraglio itself, on the left, which is completely out of keeping with the original.

Lit. H. Colvin, *Biographical Dictionary of British Architects*, 1978, pp. 126-27.
      Catalogue of the Drawings Collection of the Royal Institute of British Architects, 'B', 1972, pp. 97-98.
      J. Harris, 'Blondel at Stowe', *Connoisseur*, CLV, March 1964, p. 173.
      L. Whistler, 'Signor Borra at Stowe', *Country Life*, CXXII, 29 August 1957, p. 390.
      Information from R. Searight.

HODGES, William (1744-1797)

5 Entrance gateway to Akbar's Mausoleum, Sikandra, near Agra, India. 1786.

Inscribed *A View of the Gate of the Tomb of the Emperor Akbar at Secundrii.*
Engraved by J. Brown 1 May 1786.
Published as an illustration to W. Hodges, *Dissertation on the Prototypes of Architecture, Hindoo, Moorish and Gothic*, 1787.
Aquatint, coloured by hand. 62.5 × 46.5
British Library: India Office Library and Records (P. 2327)

William Hodges, a professional artist who made his reputation as a member of Captain Cook's party on the *Resolution* was commissioned by Warren Hastings and Augustus Cleveland to make drawings of architecture and landscape in Bengal and Upper India between 1781 and 1783. Many of these pictures were subsequently exhibited at the Royal Academy, and between 1785 and 1788 forty-eight were published under the title *Select Views in India*. Although these were not distinguished for accuracy and detail, one critic described them as 'ragged ... as if the colours were laid on the canvas with a skewer', they did convey a strong impression of the scale and grandeur of Indian architecture, and found many admirers as a result. Sir Joshua Reynolds even suggested that their 'barbaric splendour' furnished 'hints of composition and general effect' for architects to follow though he stopped short at recommending that they should be 'models to copy'.

The *Dissertation* provided a platform for Hodges to elaborate remarks which he had first made in the introductory text to the *Select Views*. Hodges's thesis was remarkable for its date in that he suggested that Hindoo and Moorish architecture were of equal importance to Classical; 'the several species of stone buildings which have been brought more or less to perfection (I mean the Egyptian, Hindoo, Moorish and Gothic architecture) instead of being copies of each other, are actually and essentially the same, the spontaneous produce of genius in different countries, the necessary effects of similar necessity and materials.' At least one architect, George Dance, a neighbour of Hodges, appears to have agreed, and the designs he produced for the façade of the Guildhall, and for Cole Orton, Leicestershire, Stratton Park, Hampshire, and other houses, all have Indian elements which have been traced to Hodges's influence.

Lit. I.C.S. Steube, *The Life and Works of William Hodges*, New York and London, 1979.
      M. Archer and R. Lightbown, *India Observed*, 1982, pp. 58-9, no. 65.
      P. Conner, *op. cit.*, pp. 113-117.

DANIELL, Thomas (1749-1840) and DANIELL, William (1769-1837)

6 Part of the Palace in the Fort of Allahabad

Plate from T. and W. Daniell *Oriental Scenery*, 1795-1808.
Lettered with title and *Drawn and engraved by Thos. Daniell. Published as the Act Directs for Thos. Daniell by Robt. Bowyer at the Historic Gallery Pall Mall September 1795.*
Aquatint, coloured by hand. Size of impression 84 × 64.
Victoria and Albert Museum (I.S. 242.8/24-1961)

Thomas Daniell and his nephew William made an extensive tour of India between April 1785 and September 1794, spending more than a year in Calcutta, visiting the north and south, and travelling by sea to the west to inspect the huge rock cut temples around Bombay. During this time they accumulated the vast collection of pictures and drawings which was to provide the material for the oil paintings and publications which occupied most of the rest of their lives. Their most famous publication, and the one which had such an extraordinary impact on the late 18th and early 19th century picturesque taste, was undoubtedly the *Oriental Scenery*, consisting of 144 aquatint engravings, which was published in parts between 1795 and 1808. Unlike the rather crude plates of Hodges, the illustrations of the Daniells combined documentary and picturesque qualities with a crisp, professional finish reminiscent of the lithographic work of many of the topographical artists of the early 19th century. Such views were readily assimilated in the late 18th century by a public eager for visual material to support the mental images conjured by romantic writers and poets.

The Daniells' plates influenced the Cockerells at Sezincote; Porden, Repton and Nash at Brighton; Edmund Aikin in *Designs for Villas and other Rural Buildings*, 1808; Thomas Hope at Duchess Street; and many other architects and designers. This particular plate, for example, is quite clearly the inspiration for the Pheasantry in H. Repton, *Designs for the Pavilion at Brighton*, 1808. Apart from the *Oriental Scenery*, the Daniells also published a number of works which were more specifically

6

architectural. *Hindoo Excavations in the Mountain of Ellora* appeared in 1803; the *Antiquities of India* a few years later, and Thomas Daniell published two views of the Taj Mahal in 1801 with a separate booklet entitled *Views of the Taje Mahel at the City of Ellora* appeared in 1803; the *Antiquities of India*, a few years later, and Thomas Daniell published two through these volumes that the British public not only gained their first glimpse of the full range of Indian building types, but also the splendour of their carved and sculpted ornament.

Not surprisingly, the Daniells also became involved in designing garden buildings after their return, and Thomas carried out various works at Melchet Park for Major Sir John Osborne, a former Indian soldier, and at Sezincote, for Sir Charles Cockerell.

Lit. P. Conner, *op. cit.*, p. 138, pl. 101.
    M. Archer and R. Lightbown, *op. cit.*.

MURPHY, James Cavanah (1760-1814)

7 Hall of the Abencerrages.

Plate in J.C. Murphy, *The Arabian Antiquities of Spain*, 1815.
Inscribed with title and *J.C. Murphy delt. Engraved by J. Shury.*
London. Published by Cadell & Davies, June 1st 1815.
Engraving. Size of impression 36.5 × 51.
Victoria and Albert Museum: National Art Library.

James Cavanah Murphy is a somewhat shadowy figure whose interests appear to have been primarily antiquarian and archaeological, but which led him, nevertheless, to produce the first important study of Islamic architecture to be published in this country. He appears to have made his first visit abroad shortly after December 1788 when the Rt. Hon. William Burton Conyngham commissioned him to make drawings of the great Dominican church and monastery at Batalha in Portugal, itself a building showing strong evidence of Eastern influence. These were subsequently published as *Plans, Elevations, Sections and Views of the Church of Batalha* (1795, 1836) and although of greatest importance in the history of the Gothic revival – William Beckford based Fonthill on the monastery – can also claim primacy in the history of the serious study of Islamic buildings. At the same time as publishing this work Murphy also published a *Voyage in Portugal* (1795).

After returning to Dublin in 1790, and moving to London shortly after, Murphy set out on another journey to the Iberian peninsula to make drawings

7

for the *Arabian Antiquities of Spain*, and to perform occasional diplomatic duties. In the introduction to the book, he records how 'the imperfect descriptions of travellers' encouraged him to make this second journey, and how he arrived at Cadiz in early May 1802. He then travelled through Lower Andalusia to Granada where 'the Governor of the Alhamra [sic] desirous that the knowledge of its splendid architectural remains should be transmitted to posterity, obligingly facilitated the author's access to that royal palace, at all hours of the day'. Later, 'equal facilities' were offered to Murphy at Cordova where he studied and drew the bridge and mosque.

Murphy remained in Spain until 1809, when he returned to London and commenced preparing his drawings for publication. Unfortunately, he died on 12 September 1814 when only a portion of the book was complete, and the *Arabian Antiquities* was published posthumously, the last part appearing on 1 June 1815. Murphy's friend T. Hartwell Horne, the antiquary and part author of Finden's *Landscape Illustrations of the Bible* (1836), supervised the completion of the work, and with John Shakespear and John Gillies wrote a *History of the Mahometan Empire* which was designed as an introduction, but was published separately in 1816.

The *Antiquities* was published by Cadell and Davies, and reproduces engravings by various artists including the Le Keux brothers, S. Porter, W. Angus, J. Stury, J. Taylor, E. Turrell and J. Fittler. The cost of hiring so many artists no doubt partly accounted for Murphy's statement that the *Antiquities* was executed at 'an expense of many thousand pounds'.

It might be wondered why this apparently meticulous volume appears in the first section of this exhibition. The reason is that Murphy's architectural scholarship was superficial. Almost from the outset the book was much criticised for its inaccuracy. Richard Ford in his excellent *Handbook for Travellers in Spain* (1845), described the plates as 'badly copied' from the *Antiguedades Arabes*, a volume of architectural drawings published by the Spaniards themselves in about 1787: 'it is difficult to believe that Murphy was ever on the spot ... the plates ... are beneath criticism from their gross inaccuracy'. Owen Jones, whose own volume on the Alhambra closely followed that of Murphy, remained studiously quiet, but Matthew Digby Wyatt in his *Industrial Arts of the Nineteenth Century* (1853) wrote that the engravings were 'sadly incorrect'.

Murphy's volume was 'a mere book making job', not a serious attempt to understand the Alhambra and its decoration. Nevertheless, it undoubtedly served to direct public attention to Spanish architecture for the first time, and in scale at least, may be likened to the publications of the architects in the second section of the exhibition.

Lit. *Dictionary of National Biography.*
   Catalogue of the Drawings Collection of the Royal Institute of British Architects, L-N, 1973, p. 99.

PAGE, William (1794-1872)

8 Fountain of Bab-Houmayon, Istanbul. c. 1824
Water-colour. 82 × 55.8
Searight Collection

William Page studied at the Royal Academy schools under Fuseli and appears to have travelled to the Near East visiting Turkey and Greece in the early 1820s. Certainly he had returned to England by 1824, when he exhibited this drawing at the Royal Academy under the title 'Fountain of Azal, Dgiamici, or of Ybrahim Bey Oglon, Constantinople' (no. 893), and gave his address as 23 Argyle Street, St. Pancras. In the following year he exhibited a companion picture 'Fountain of Tophana' (no. 550). Both pictures were produced as aquatints by J. Bailey and R. Reeve for Ackermann in 1829. Other drawings made by Page on his tour were redrawn by professional topographical draughtsmen for engravings in Finden's *Landscape and Portrait Illustrations to the Life and Works of Lord Byron* (1833-34) and *Landscape Illustrations of the Bible* (1836); and a set of figure studies of Turks, Greeks and Albanians, on paper watermarked between 1810 and 1822, is also in the Searight Collection.

Page's drawing illustrates the Ahmed III fountain in Istanbul, built as late as 1728 when Turkish architecture shows strong evidence of French influence. Like most artists of the 18th and early 19th centuries his concern was apparently with the picturesque rather than the historically interesting.

Lit. J.H. Money, 'The Life and Work of William Page', *Annual,* of the Old Water Colour Society's Club, 47, 1972, pp. 9-30.
   Information from R. Searight.

PORDEN, William (c.1775-1822)

9 Interior of the stables, Royal Pavilion, Brighton. 1803-8
Plate 26 in *Views of the Royal Pavilion,* 1826, published by John Nash and Rudolph Ackermann. This plate etched by John Cleghorn after Charles Moore.
Museum and Art Gallery, Brighton.

Porden started his architectural career as a pupil of James Wyatt in 1774 and shortly after moved to the office of Samuel Pepys Cockerell. In 1797 he showed a 'design for a Place of Public Amusement, in the style of Mahometan Architecture in Hindostan' at the Royal Academy (no. 1136) and perhaps it was this design, or a scheme of a few years later for the remodelling of Eaton Hall, Cheshire, for the 2nd Earl of Grosvenor in the 'Morisco Gothic' style, which persuaded the Prince Regent to build a new stables and riding house at Brighton. Certainly neither Brighton Pavilion itself, nor the Cockerells' Sezincote had been conceived when the stables were begun in 1803. Perhaps the Arab stallion itself was the immediate inspiration. Whatever the case, Porden's colossal domed rotunda and barrel vaulted Riding House encompassing an area of 10,000 square feet, certainly pleased the Prince, for the exotic character of the Pavilion itself was inspired by them.

Conner, who has studied the Faringdon diaries, notes that Porden's inspiration for the stables were 'on his own admission, modelled on the Halle au Blé in Paris, a cylindrical cornmarket which received a shallow wooden dome in 1782 and then lost it in a fire in 1803. But the proportions and range of sizes of the scallop-arched windows in the stables appear to follow the Jami Masjid or Great Mosque at Delhi of which a view was engraved by the Daniells and published in 1797.'

The stables, now known as the Dome, were converted in 1867 into an Assembly Room and remodelled internally in 1934-5 as a concert hall. The Riding House was later used as a Corn Exchange and is now an Exhibition Hall.

Lit. Colvin, *op. cit.,* p. 653.
   P. Conner, *op. cit.,* pp. 131-36, pl. 93.
   H.D. Roberts, *History of the Royal Pavilion,* Brighton, 1939.

COCKERELL, Samuel Pepys (c.1754-1827)

10 The south front and the greenhouse pavilion, Sezincote House, Gloucestershire. c.1805
Modern photography courtesy of *Country Life.*

Sezincote was built by Sir Charles Cockerell and his brother Samuel Pepys, who acted as architect, between 1805 and 1810. Charles Cockerell had acquired considerable wealth in India, and wishing 'to introduce the gardening and architecture' which he had seen there to England, apparently consulted,

8

9

10

in about 1805, Humphry Repton. Repton, who was then in the process of working on his designs for the Royal Pavilion at Brighton, records in his book on the Pavilion published in 1808, that the idea of building in the Indian style was new to him, and that he recommended that Cockerell consult the drawings of Thomas Daniell. Meanwhile, Samuel Pepys Cockerell had already decorated the interior of nearby Daylesford House in the Indian taste and was, thus, already familiar with the style, and perhaps with the work of Daniell. It is tempting to surmise that he may also have been in contact with his old friend William Porden whose stables at Brighton had started building in the previous year. Certainly both men chose to adopt the Mughal, Islamic style rather than the Hindoo, though the ease with which the former could be adapted to English requirements no doubt much encouraged this.

With the exception of the dairy, which was described as Moorish rather than Mughal, the Indianisation of Sezincote ceases abruptly on entering the front door. The 18th and early 19th century English gentleman could live with Moghul buildings and enjoy their picturesque qualities, but he could not live in them. Sezincote is perhaps the most successful of the Islamic buildings of this date. The carefully contrived masses of golden Stanway stone, skilfully articulated with crisply carved details, form an excellent substitute for the red sand stone of Delhi and Agra, and contrast well with the luxuriant 'Indian' landscaping, with its bridge and temple to the Hindu goddess Souriya, designed by

Thomas Daniell. In the sense that the exotic quality of the house is culled from a single source and is not the result of the mixing of Far Eastern, Gothic and Indian styles, as for example at Brighton, Cockerell's work looks forward to the early Victorian period and its concern for archaeological accuracy.

Lit. C. Hussey, *English Country Houses, Late Georgian 1800-1840*, 1958, pp. 66-73.
P. Conner, *op. cit.*, pp. 120-127.

MARTIN, John (1789-1854)

11 The Fall of Nineveh. 1830.
Signed and dated *J. Martin 1829*. Lettered with title, dedication to King Charles X of France and *Painted & Engraved by John Martin. London. Published July 1 1830 by Mr Martin. 30 Allsops Terrace, New Road.*
Mezzotint, coloured by hand. 91.1 × 66.7
Victoria and Albert Museum (E. 567-1968)

This engraving is based on an oil painting of the same title which was begun in the autumn of 1827, and exhibited at the Western Exchange in May of the following year. It was larger than any of Martin's previous pictures and contained 'more figures, more buildings and more movement'. He explained in a printed catalogue which accompanied the picture: 'The mighty cities of Nineveh and Babylon have long since passed away. The accounts of their greatness and splendour may have been exaggerated. But, where strict truth is not essential, the mind is content to find delight in the contemplation of the grand and marvellous. Into the solemn visions of antiquity we look without demanding the clear daylight of truth. Seen through the mist of ages, the *great* become *gigantic*, the *wonderful* swells into the *sublime* ... The Style of architecture, partaking of the Egyptian on the one hand, and of the most ancient Indian on the other, has been invented as the most appropriate for a city situate between the two countries, and necessarily in frequent intercourse with them.'

Martin's statement further emphasises what little information about Near Eastern architecture was available in the 1820s. He had to fall back upon Indian sources in order to validate the essentially Egyptian form of his buildings. He had made a set of ten etchings of Sezincote for Sir Charles Cockerell in the autumn of 1817, and must surely have known the illustrations of the Daniells, of which Cockerell owned examples, so that he was to a certain extent familiar with Indian buildings. But what conveys a Near Eastern impression in his work is not so much the architecture, which is more convincingly early Victorian than Persian – Bonomi's Marshall's Mill at Leeds writ large – as his mixing of Biblical sources

with the imagery of the *Arabian Nights*. Indeed, so successful is this that when the young Disraeli looked upon Jerusalem for the first time in 1831, he considered it would be 'a wonderful subject for Martin and a picture from him could alone give you an idea of it'.

Interestingly, by the 1830s Martin was closely involved with Joseph Bonomi and Henry Warren, who feature in later sections of this exhibition, and who could have provided him with the Near Eastern detail which he lacked in the 20s. Bonomi married Martin's daughter Jessie, twenty-nine years his junior, and when she died in childbirth in 1859, Martin's other daughter, Isabella, brought up the Bonomis' four surviving children, and also took over the running of the Soane Museum with their father. Bonomi's friend Henry Warren, whose well known portrait of Martin is in the National Portrait Gallery, married the daughter of Martin's sister, who lived with Martin during most of the 1830s. Later, Warren's son Albert Henry, the pupil of Owen Jones, worked with Martin on his utopian schemes for the Thames Embankments.

Lit. T. Balston, *John Martin 1789-1854 His Life and Works*, 1947.
     R. Blake, *Disraeli's Grand Tour*, 1982, p. 66.

11

SECTION 2

ISLAMIC ARCHITECTURE   DELINEATED

Hard on the heels of the early grand tourists who visited the Near East followed many of the young men who, on their return to England, were to become leading architects of the Victorian period. Some, like Charles Cockerell, Thomas Leverton Donaldson and Lewis Vulliamy travelled to Turkey overland from Greece. Cockerell records in his *Journal* that he visited Constantinople in 1810 and did drawings there, 'of palaces, serais, etc., but the difficulty and really the danger I have had to incur to do them you would not believe'.[1] He had little respect for the native buildings: 'To architecture in the highest sense, viz. elegant construction in stone, the Turks have no pretension. The mosques are always copies of Santa Sophia with trifling variations, and have no claim to originality!' Like many of those who visited Constantinople before him, he found the fountains and kiosks most interesting. They were the only 'really ornamental buildings in which anything that may be called Turkish architecture is displayed', and on his return to England he showed a drawing he had made while staying in Janina of a kiosk, at the Royal Academy (fig. 3). Vulliamy and Donaldson visited the city shortly after Cockerell and also found little to interest them architecturally, although Vulliamy did a number of sensitive drawings of mosques, of which two are included in the exhibition (nos. 12 and 13).

One architect who visited Constantinople at this time, Charles Barry, continued his travels south to Egypt. He had been about to return to England with his companions Charles Lock Eastlake and William Kinnaird, when David Baillie, an archaeologist from Cambridge, who had admired Barry's drawings in Athens, offered to take him to Egypt and Syria, and to pay £200 a year for his sketches. Barry's drawings are now in the Griffith Institute at Oxford and consist mainly of views of ancient Egyptian sites; Islamic architecture did not, it seems, particularly interest him.

Baillie was perhaps induced to travel to Egypt as a result of the discovery and publication of so many of the ancient sites by the French. The famous *Description de l'Egypte* (1809-1828), Denon's *Voyage dans la Basse et la Haute Egypte* (1802), and many other volumes were certainly very influential

in persuading travellers and particularly architects, to visit there. Unlike Charles Barry, most travelled directly to Alexandria by sea from Sicily or Malta. Joseph John Scoles, Henry Parke and Frederick Catherwood, who travelled down the Nile together in 1823-4, for example, chose this route.

All travellers to the ancient sites prepared for their journeys in Cairo, and it was apparently there that the first real awakening of interest in Islamic architecture took place. Contemporary descriptions of Cairene houses give some indication of their picturesque qualities and extraordinary fascination. Thackeray's account of his visit to the painter John Frederick Lewis (no. 46) is a good example. Unlike the colossal monuments along the banks of the Nile, Cairene buildings were more domestic in scale, and to architects whose main concern was the design of houses rather than tombs, this no doubt added to their appeal. Obituaries of James William Wild, who lived in Cairo in the 1840s, make clear that this was certainly the interest for him (nos. 42-45). Another attraction was undoubtedly the fact that such buildings had not been the subject of previous study before. Pascal Coste's extraordinarily detailed drawings (no. 15) adhere to the same pattern of meticulous draughtsmanship and careful observation which distinguishes many 18th century books devoted to classical buildings. Volumes like those of Coste not only conveyed new information but helped to establish reputations, which was an important consideration for young architects at the outset of their careers, when no examinations in the modern sense existed to quickly establish individual merit.

But, perhaps the most fascinating feature of Cairene buildings, and of Islamic architecture in general, was the extraordinarily emotive atmosphere which the rich decoration and intricate sculpture evoked. This was outside the range of experience for which classical teaching at the Royal Academy and elsewhere had prepared most architects, and as a result, opened their eyes to effects of colour and ornament which had been ignored for centuries. In their desire to understand and record this there is, perhaps, a parallel with the work of artists like John Bourne, whose illustrations of the Great Western Railway succeeded so

Figure 3

Figure 4

Figure 5

brilliantly in making art out of the new technology. Both schools were concerned with the specific rather than the general, and their work heralds a new age in which documentation became an element of the picturesque.

One of the most important contributory factors to the Eastern experience was undoubtedly polychromy – the Islamic architects use of combinations of bright colours. Neo-Classicism had introduced to England an architecture that was peculiarly white. Although some travellers had returned from Greece clutching coloured fragments of classical buildings, and although Stuart and Revett, Edward Dodwell and many other authors depict plates showing evidence of painted decoration on various classical buildings, including the Parthenon, neo-classical architects steadfastly ignored this, and continued to advocate the use of white painted stucco façades articulated with three dimensional ornamentation rather than colour.[2] They tended to treat the evidence of polychromy as an archaeological curiosity, or as an indication of barbarism during the Middle Ages. No one appears to have accepted the wider aesthetic and philosophical implications of Greek polychromy; no one attempted to analyse the evidence from different sources to ascertain whether it adhered to particular principles; and above all, no one before 1820 attempted to re-construct a classical building with its polychromy restored.

It is, therefore, against this background that the work of the first architects to study Islamic buildings and decoration must be seen. We know that Jules Goury, Gottfried Semper's travelling companion in Greece and joint author with Owen Jones of *Plans,*

Details, Elevations and Sections of the Alhambra (1842-5) (nos. 32-37), had become interested in Islamic colour after first studying Greek buildings, for Semper, in a footnote in his *Die Vier Elemente der Baukunst* (1851), noted that Goury's portfolio 'must contain the most complete and most reliable collection on polychromy that exists'.[3] Similarly, Ludwig Zanth who built the Moorish Villa Wilhelma for the King of Württemberg from 1837 (no. 53), had been studying polychromatic buildings in Sicily in the 1820s with Jacob Ignaz Hittorff. Their *Architecture Antique de la Sicile* (1827) was one of the first volumes to establish beyond all doubt that the classical temples had been brilliantly painted. The writer of Owen Jones's obituary in the *Builder* remembered that he had heard Jones speak of the effect produced upon him by his first view of Italy from the Great St. Bernard Pass: 'his eye for colour was opening, and in walking afterwards over Sicily his taste was more and more developed in that direction.'

Where Goury, Zanth, and Jones, and their contemporaries Girault de Prangey (nos. 38, 39) and Charles Texier (nos. 40, 41) differed from writers like Stuart and Revett, and Dodwell, was that instead of simply noting the coloured remains, they made painstaking studies of them. To thrill to the colours was not enough, the ancient systems of polychromatic decoration had to be analysed in detail, for only in that way could similar effects be reproduced in contemporary works. It was with the specific intention of pursuing this interest further that Jones and Goury, who met in Egypt in 1832, decided to travel north to Constantinople and thence, by sea, to Spain to visit the Alhambra. In making their surveys, however, they encountered a problem which was fundamental to all early polychromatic studies; the paucity of coloured remains and the difficulty of interpreting them.

Many vestiges of paint were still to be seen on the walls of the Alhambra, but they required careful study in so far as they had either faded or oxidised, or were the work of later restorers. 'The grounds of many of the ornaments are found to be green; in all cases however, it will be seen, on minute examination that the colour originally employed was blue, which being a metallic colour, has become green from the effects of time.'[5] Although the shafts of the columns throughout the Alhambra bore no traces of colour, Jones and Goury decided that they had been gilded: 'the harmony of the colouring appears to require that they should be gilt.' They maintained that the Spanish kings had found it simpler to remove the gilt from the shafts than to incur the cost of regilding: 'that they were allowed to remain white originally no one can suppose who will for an instant mentally restore the colouring.' Such statements are surprising in the context of so meticulous and accurate a study, particularly since at least one of the Arabic inscriptions on the walls of the Alhambra, which Jones had had translated by the Arabic scholar Pasqual de Gayangos, referred to columns: 'which when struck by the rays of the rising sun, one might fancy not withstanding their colossal dimensions to be so many blocks of pearl.'

The architects like Hittorff and Semper who sought to rationalise Greek architectural polychromy encountered more fundamental problems, for much less colour survived than on the Alhambra. The polychromatic reconstructions of the Parthenon and other buildings which they made in the 1820s and 30s reveal several quite distinct schools of thought with, at the two extremes, the theories of Franz Kugler who believed that the Greeks used colour simply to highlight the aesthetic beauty of marble, and at the other, the ideas of Semper who believed that every inch of the marble had been completely covered with paint and gilding. Seen in this context, the work of the Islamic 'revivalists' places them firmly with the school which believed in 'all over' polychromy.

The concern about colour expressed by these architects was specific in the sense that it involved architecture and architectural decoration, yet topical in the context of the romantic movement as a whole, when polychromy also taxed the minds of artists, writers and scientists. Turner, for example, who had accompanied Donaldson in Italy, experimented with the immaterial qualities of colour, many of his pictures conveying effects analogous to the architectural and landscape experiences described by travellers to the Near East. At the same time, the exuberant primaries of Delacroix and John Frederick Lewis support their involvement with the passions underlying so much fictional writing about the Orient in the late 18th and early 19th century. Lewis's palette changed completely as a result of his first visit to Spain, green and brown washes being replaced by much brighter colours. John Sell Cotman, seeing several hundred of his drawings, wrote in a letter to his friend

Dawson Turner on 6 January 1834: 'Words cannot convey to you their splendour. My poor *Reds, Blues and Yellows* – for which I have been in Norwich much abused and broken-hearted about are *faded fades* to what I saw there.'[6] The work of the scientists on colour is described in more detail in the next section.

The work of artists like Lewis, David Roberts, Thomas Allom (no. 47) and William Henry Bartlett (no. 48), although not primarily architectural in the sense of that of Pascal Coste or James Wild, or even of James Murphy, was nevertheless, an important facet of the interest of the 1830s and 40s in Islamic buildings. Like the earlier topographical prints of William Hodges and Thomas and William Daniell, the volumes of lithographs and engravings which they published were not only influential in their own right, but also provided a visual context into which the plans and elevations of the architects could be fitted. Indeed, one cannot help wondering to what extent the success of their work may have helped to mitigate against the acceptance of the Islamic style in Britain later in the century, simply by ensuring that it always looked out of place.

John Frederick Lewis and David Roberts travelled to Spain in 1832-33, just a few years after Sir David Wilkie (to whom Washington Irving dedicated his *Alhambra* in 1832), and a few months before Owen Jones and Jules Goury. Although they frequently covered the same ground, Lewis and Roberts never met. Lewis arrived at the Alhambra late in 1832, and returned there in the spring of the following year. In the meantime he had made a trip to Seville, where he had stayed with Richard Ford (then busy compiling his well known *Handbook for Travellers to Spain* (1845)) and had visited Gibraltar. The products of Lewis's travels were the popular *Sketches and Drawings of the Alhambra* (1835) and *Sketches of Spain and Spanish Character* (1836), publications which earned for him the title of 'Spanish Lewis'. Roberts arrived at the Alhambra shortly after Lewis left for Seville. He had visited Burgos and Madrid on the way, before moving to Cordova where he spent three weeks making drawings of the mosque and bridge, and other buildings. But, if he found the Hispano-Moresque architecture of Cordova attractive, he was enthralled by the Alhambra, writing home that: 'Courts, halls, terraces, galleries and fountains out of number are here, and golden fish still desport themselves in the numerous ponds. The gardens are filled with orange and lemon trees laden with fruit, and even at this early season the flowers are in full bloom and beauty.'[7] At the same time he received a letter from Lewis confessing that when he had visited the building he had 'regretted then for the first time in my life that I did not draw architecture, and almost intended to commence, but as you are there now, lucky man am I who let it alone.'[8] Roberts subsequently visited Gibraltar too, but then extended his journey further south to Tangier and Tetuan, before travelling home via Cadiz, Jerez and Seville. The fruits of his tour were not only many illustrations for the *Landscape Annuals*, and pictures shown at the Royal Academy and elsewhere, but also a volume of lithographs entitled

Picturesque Sketches in Spain (1837), and a Diorama of the Court of the Lions at the Alhambra intended for the Royal Bazaar in Oxford Street.

Inspired by their experiences in Spain, both artists travelled to the Near East too. The story of Roberts's journey in 1838-39 is told in detail in his journals, edited by James Ballantine as *The Life of David Roberts* (1867), and is illustrated by the five vast volumes of lithographs he published after his return entitled *The Holy Land, Syria, Idumea, Arabia, Egypt and Nubia* (1842-49). Lewis stayed in Egypt longer, living in Cairo for almost ten years to make the hundreds of sketches and drawings which became the basis for the well known water-colours he painted after his return.

Roberts's drawings, like those of Thomas Allom and William Bartlett, were in particular demand to illustrate volumes with biblical themes such as Finden's *Landscape Illustrations of the Bible* (136-39) or Bartlett's *In the Footsteps of Our Lord and His Apostles in Syria, Greece and Italy* (1851). Such books were popular in the Victorian era, and scholarly interest in biblical history, as an aspect of the religious revival of that period, must be considered another important factor in the preoccupation with the Near East with which this exhibition is concerned. The first systematic work on the archaeology of the Holy Land was carried out by the American historian Dr Edward Robinson, and his book *Biblical Researches in Palestine, Mount Sinai and Arabia Petraea* (1841) was held in considerable respect by the architects who feature here. Further East, in Mesopotamia, the work of Paul Botta and Eugene Flandin led to the publication of their *Monuments de Ninive* (1849-50), while that of Austen Layard at Nimrud led to the assembling of the great Assyrian collections at the British Museum and the publication of his *Nineveh and its Remains* (1850), and other related volumes.

Layard had been wandering through Asia Minor and Syria in the autumn and winter of 1838-39, when he 'felt an irresistible desire to penetrate to the regions beyond the Euphrates, to which history and tradition point as the birthplace of the wisdom of the West.'[9] It was a similar compulsion which drove Frederick Catherwood, at great personal risk, to enter the Dome of the Rock in Jerusalem, in 1833

(nos 19, 20). In the context of this exhibition, Catherwood's was the most interesting of the 'excavations' bearing on biblical history, for the Dome of the Rock was not only built on the site of Solomon's Temple, parts of which it was thought may have been incorporated, but it was also the first great monument of Islamic architecture (fig. 5). Of all the buildings in the Near East the Dome of the Rock received more attention than any other in the 19th century, with the possible exception of S. Sophia in Constantinople. Catherwood, Arundale and Bonomi's meticulous measured drawings remained largely unpublished and, consequently, unknown, so that curiosity about the appearance of the mosque persisted throughout the century. On 1st December 1857 when the Reverend A.A. Isaacs published his *Four Views of the Mosques and other Objects of Interest Occupying the Site of the Temple at Jerusalem* he erroneously declared that 'no views of these structures have ever been obtained or published before', and his text conveys the excitement he felt in revealing them to the British public for the first time.

Subsequent volumes such as James Fergusson's *The Ancient Topography of Jerusalem* (1849) or Thomas Hayter Lewis's *The Holy Places of Jerusalem* (1888) (nos. 21, 22) attempted to disentangle the complex history of the Dome of the Rock and its site, and thus went further than the work of the 1830s which was primarily concerned with recording its appearance. Like Gaspard Fossati's restoration of Santa Sophia in 1847,[10] in which he was concerned to distinguish the Byzantine fabric from later Islamic additions (and was closely watched by the Western architectural world as he did so), Fergusson and Lewis sought to isolate earlier work from that commissioned by 'Abd al-Malik in 691. The task was complicated by the fact that much Islamic building inevitably involved a fusion of cultural elements. The Dome of the Rock, for example, was essentially 'Western' in plan with a domed rotunda and ambulatories, but included Hellenistic (Persian-Sasanian) influence in the stone carving and mosaic decorations. Their attempt to understand the nature of these disparate elements marks the beginning of the modern chapter of Islamic architectural research, when interpretation may be said to have succeeded delineation.

Notes

1 *Travels in Southern Europe and the Levant, 1810-17. The Journal of C.R. Cockerell, R.A.,* edited by S.P. Cockerell, 1903, pp. 26-30, this and subsequent quotations.
2 D. van Zanten, *The Architectural Polychromy of the 1830s,* 1977, includes numerous references to classical polychromy after 1750.
3 I am grateful to Dr W. Hermann for pointing out this footnote to me.
4 *Builder* 9 May 1874, p. 383.
5 O. Jones and J. Goury, *Alhambra,* letterpress to plate XXXVIII.
6 Quoted by S.D. Kitson, *The Life of John Sell Cotman,* 1937, p. 306.
7 Quoted by F. Irwin in *Artist Adventurer David Roberts 1796-1864,* Scottish Arts Council, 1981, p. 12.
8 *ibid.,* pp. 11-12.
9 Quoted by C.W. Ceram, *Gods, Graves and Scholars,* 1979, p. 261.
10 See *Aya Sofia Constantinople, As recently restored by Order of H.M. Sultan Abdvl Medjid, from the original drawings by Chevalier Gaspard Fossati.* Lithographed by Louis Haghe Esq., 1852.

VULLIAMY, Lewis (1791-1871)

**12 View of the Yeni Valide Camii, Istanbul, with a
sketch detail and plan. c.1818.**
Inscribed with title and numbered 5. The paper is watermarked *J.
Green 1812*.
Pencil. 26.3 × 41.9.
Searight Collection.

13

13 View of the Şehzade Camii, Istanbul. c.1818.
Inscribed with title and *Sultan Suleiman* deleted.
Pencil. 42 × 26.7.
Searight Collection.

Until recently when these and other drawings appeared in the sale room, it was not known that Lewis Vulliamy had made studies of Islamic buildings on his grand Tour. The volume which he published on his return, *Examples of Ornamental Sculpture in Architecture from Greece, Asia Minor and Italy* (1825), is exclusively devoted to classical subjects, and although obituaries note that he refused to allow aesthetic prejudices to interfere with his practice, and that he worked with equal facility in a number of styles, nothing designed or written by him suggests an interest in Islamic art. That he had studied the Yeni Valide Camii is interesting because it may have been partly as a result of his experiences and these drawings, that Owen Jones, who was articled to Vulliamy from 1824, visited the city in 1833 with Jules Goury, and also made drawings of this particular mosque (see nos. 26, 27).

The Yeni Valide Camii, often called simply the Yeni Cami, or New Mosque, was designed by Davut Ağa for the Valide Sultan Safiye, mother of Mehmet III, and partly built between 1597 and 1603, when Mehmet died and work stopped. After lying derelict for many years it was finally completed in 1663. The Şehzade Camii was built by Sinan in 1544-8 for

Sultan Süleyman. The two mosques are, therefore, among the most interesting of the Islamic buildings in Istanbul, because of their comparatively early date.

Lit. H. Colvin, *op. cit.*, pp. 857-58.
      Builder, 25 February 1871, p. 142.

BONOMI, Joseph (1796-1878); SCOLES, Joseph John (1798-1863) and HAY, Robert (1799-1863)

14 Letter from Joseph Bonomi in Derr, Egypt to Joseph John Scoles in Rome, dated May 2, 1825.
Private Collection.

This letter serves to introduce three travellers to the Near East all of whom drew Islamic buildings at one time or another, but whose main interest in the context of this exhibition lies in their involvement with the other architects and artists featured. Scoles and Bonomi had left England together in 1822 for Italy. After visiting Rome Bonomi remained behind while Scoles continued to Egypt, where in company with Henry Parke and Frederick Catherwood he made a journey down the Nile. Immediately after this he travelled north to Jerusalem when he prepared the plan, published in 1825, which was later used by Catherwood, Arundale and Bonomi (see nos. 19-23). After returning to England, Scoles became Secretary of the Royal Institute of British

Architects and was one of the founder members of the Syro-Egyptian Society.

It has been said that it was study of Catherwood's Egyptian drawings that first induced Robert Hay, the wealthy 'Laird of Linplum', to mount the first of the Egyptian expeditions with which his name is so enduringly linked. Whatever the case, he was certainly looking for artists to accompany him by 1824, for Bonomi explains in this letter to Scoles, how after Scoles had left him in Rome, he had 'got into all sorts of trouble ... got robbed and because abandoned to all sorts of vices ... was induced to accept Mr Hay's offer which I must now tell you is little enough (entre nous) £50 a year and he is to have all the original drawings.' Bonomi soon found Hay 'to be a *Scot* and not one of those who have a bellyful of learning;' furthermore, he was 'one of the most ignorant men I ever met excessively purse proud and extremely rich.' In spite of these sanctions Bonomi remained associated with Hay for many years, and with James Haliburton (called Burton, the brother of Decimus Burton), Charles Laver, Edward Lane, J.G. Wilkinson, G.B. Greenough, George Hoskins, Francis Arundale and Frederick Catherwood, all of whom were members of Hay's expeditions at one time or another, they laid down the basis of Egyptian archaeology as we know it today.

Lit. J.J. Scoles, 'On the Topography and Antiquities of the City of Jerusalem', *Builder*, 24 February 1849, pp. 88-91.
Builder, 16 January 1864, p. 41.
S. Tillett, *The Laird of Linplum*, manuscript biography of Robert Hay.

COSTE, Pascal Xavier (1787-1879)

15 Volume of original drawings for the artist's *Architecture Arabe, ou Monuments du Kaire*, Paris, 1837-9.
Pencil, pen and ink, and water-colour. Sixty-one sheets each 44.5 × 58.
Searight Collection.

Coste's magnificent volume was the most detailed study of the architecture of Cairo to be published in the 19th century and undoubtedly had great influence. Surely it cannot have been a coincidence, for example, that Léon Vaudoyer's Marseilles Cathedral, with its striped stonework, minarets, and other Islamic – particularly Cairene – features, should have been built in Coste's home city from 1845 while he lived there. Certainly Coste's autobiography records many meetings with Vaudoyer.

Interestingly, this volume of drawings was purchased from Coste by Robert Hay during the latter's first expedition. Tillett records in his unpublished biography of Hay that Coste 'had offered Hay very reasonable terms for the exclusive rights to all his own notes and drawings on condition of their publication no later than 1830.' But Hay's 'remarkable lack of application and financial sense', which was to become a recurrent theme of the remainder of his life, meant that he procrastinated, and as a group of letters from August 1828 to November 1829 in the Bodleian Library reveal, Coste was obliged to enter into a series of complex negotiations with him in which Edward Lane acted as middleman. Originally Coste and Lane had both offered to superintend the engraving of the drawings, but Hay had declined to enter into arrangements with a publisher until he possessed Coste's notes too. Coste threatened to publish copies of the drawings which he had made before selling them to Hay, but Lane advised Hay to register the copyright in his own name, and Coste immediately recanted by sending Hay his notes on three of the Cairo mosques. After further delays negotiations finally broke down completely. Lane, who had taken over the task of finding a publisher, was unsuccessful, even after Coste had agreed to extend his deadline to August 1831 (provided Hay supplied him with five free copies), and Coste was eventually obliged to publish the book himself using his copy drawings.

In 1836 Hay considered including some of Coste's drawings in his *Views in Cairo*, but after hearing rumour of the impending publication of Coste's own work, he lent the whole volume of drawings to Edward Lane who used it to assist William Harvey in preparing the illustrations for his *Arabian Nights* (no. 65).

Lit. S. Tillett, *op. cit.*, pp. 63-66, 100.
P. Coste, *Notes et Souvenirs de Voyages*, Marseilles 1878.
Information from R. Searight.

CARTER, Owen Browne (1806-1859)

16 A street in Cairo near the Bab El-Khark.
Plate in R. Hay, *Views in Cairo*, 1840.
Inscribed with title and *On stone by J.C. Bourne, from a drawing by Owen B. Carter Archt. Printed by C. Hullmandel*
Lithograph. 36.6 × 50
Private Collection.

On 15 July 1829 Robert Hay commissioned the artist Charles Laver to join his Egyptian expedition. Laver in turn recommended that Carter, who was his friend, should accompany him and the two men set out for Cairo arriving sometime after 1 October 1829. After several months in the city when Carter appears to have completed most of his drawings, the expedition finally set off up the Nile, spending four months at Beni Hasan and el Amarna, before moving to Siout. At Siout both Laver and Carter became ill, and Carter was obliged to return home via Cairo.

Several years later, after Hay himself had also returned, he determined to publish the Cairo drawings and he contacted Carter in April 1836, sending him a number of views to copy for printing. This was against the advice of his friend Edward Lane who recommended, rather surprisingly in view of Carter's background: 'whoever draws them on stone should of course have the original outlines to assist him. Mr Carter evidently does not understand some of the architectural details.' Although the volume was to contain picturesque views, Hay's advisers were very anxious that they should be accurate. Lane did not trust Hay to write the introductory text and sent him an example of what he thought should be said which makes the

15

16

point clearly. 'No work on Egypt, hitherto published, presents a collection of pictorial illustrations of its Temples & Tombs (with their sculptures & painting, its Modern Public & Private Edifices, & its Scenery, sufficiently comprehensive and accurate to satisfy even those who take an ordinary interest in such subjects. Most of the views in the great 'Description de l'Egypte' are extremely inaccurate & the splendid & valuable works of Rosellini & Champollion are almost exclusively adapted to the student of Archaeology. It is therefore, proposed to offer to the Public a series of views etc. suited at once to the wants of the Antiquary, the Architect, & the Lover of the Picturesque, & serving to elucidate the description both of ancient and modern authors'.

After various vicissitudes and delays during which other artists became involved, including Henry Warren who added the figures to Carter's drawings, and Owen Jones who designed and printed the coloured title page (no. 62), the volume finally appeared on 30 November 1840. Unfortunately for Hay it did not sell well and he lost heavily over it.

Lit. S. Tillett, op. cit., pp. 99-105. A detailed account of the volume from which the above is taken.
   Athenaeum, 26 December 1840, p. 1028.

ARUNDALE, Francis Vyvyan Jago (1807-1853)

17 Plan, elevation and details of the fountain for ablution in the cortile of the Mosque of Mourad Bey, Cairo. c.1833.
Lettered with title and *Plan. Section. Console at Large. Open Woodwork of Roof. Line of roof.* Scales *.001pm* and *.002pm*.
Pencil and water-colour. 20.3 × 25.5.
Searight Collection.

17

18

18 The Palace of the Cadi, Cairo. c.1833.
Inscribed with title.
Pencil and water-colour. 25.1 × 20.
Searight Collection.

Francis Arundale had studied under Augustus
Pugin before joining Robert Hay's second Egyptian
Expedition in 1832. Subsequently he remained in
the Near East for nine years, and then travelled home
via Greece and Sicily. Arundale produced a number
of magnificent water-colour landscapes for Robert
Hay, as well as many detailed reconstructions of
temple façades which are now in the British
museum (Add Ms 29846). Although impressive in
execution, however, the latter have been criticised
as 'not very strong evidence of what actually
existed'.

Arundale suffered from epilepsy and the
accounts of Bonomi, Catherwood and others contain
frequent references to his fits. While visiting
Jerusalem with Bonomi and Catherwood in 1833, for
example, Bonomi recorded in his diary 'poor
Arundale fell down we ... applied our usual remedy,
cold water thrown from a height on his head ... at 12
o'clock another attack'.

Lit. *Art Journal*, 1854, p. 50.
   Builder, 1854, p. 83.
   S. Tillett, *op. cit.*, pp. 73-75.

CATHERWOOD, Frederick (1799-1854)

19 W.H. Bartlett, *Walks about the City and
Environs of Jerusalem*, **1842, pp. 148-151, 'Mr
Catherwood's Adventure'.**
Victoria and Albert Museum: National Art Library

20 The Dome of the Rock, Jerusalem.
Plate in *Landscape Illustrations of the Bible*, engraved by W. and
E. Finden, volume I, 1836.
Lettered with title [incorrectly] and *Drawn by D. Roberts from a
sketch by F. Catherwood. Engraved by E. Finden. London.
Published 1835 by John Murray.*
Engraving on India Paper. 30 × 23.4.
Searight Collection.

Victor von Hagen notes that until 1833 The Dome of
the Rock in Jerusalem had not been measured or
drawn; 'no architect up to that time had ever
sketched its architecture, no antiquarian had traced
its interior design ... unbelievers took their lives in
their hands when they entered those sacred portals'.
On 13 November in that year, however, Frederick
Catherwood, who was visiting Jerusalem with his
friends Joseph Bonomi and Francis Arundale,
dressed up as an Egyptian officer, and accompanied
by an Egyptian servant 'of great courage and
assurance', entered the buildings of the Mosque
with his drawing materials feeling 'irresistibly
urged to make an attempt to explore them'. In a letter

20

quoted by W.H. Bartlett, Catherwood explained what happened: 'It was a proceeding certain to attract attention and expose me to dangerous consequences. The cool assurance of my servant, at once befriended and led me on. We entered, and arranging the camera [lucida] I quickly sat down to work, not without some nervousness, as I perceived the Mussulmen, from time to time, mark me with doubtful looks; however, most of them passed on, deceived by my dress and the quiet indifference with which I regarded them. At length, some more fanatic than the rest, began to think all could not be right; they gathered at a distance in groups, suspiciously eyeing me, and comparing notes with one another; a storm was evidently gathering. They approached, broke into sudden clamour and surrounding us, uttered loud curses: their numbers increased most alarmingly, and with their numbers their menacing language and gestures. Escape was hopeless; I was completely surrounded by a mob of two hundred people, who seemed screwing up their courage for a sudden rush upon me – I need not tell you what would have been my fate. Nothing could be better than the conduct of Suleyman, my servant, at this crisis; affecting vast indignation at the interruption, he threatened to inform the Governor, out-hectored the most clamorous, and raising his whip, actually commenced a summary attack upon them, and knocked off the cap of one of the holy dervishes. This brought matters to a crisis; and, I believe, few moments would have passed ere we had been torn to pieces, when an incident occurred

36

that converted our danger and discomfiture into positive triumph. This was the sudden appearance of the Governor on the steps of the platform, accompanied by his usual train. Catching sight of him, the foremost, – those I mean who had been disgraced by the blows of Suleyman – rushed tumultuously up to him, demanding the punishment of the infidel, who was profaning the holy precincts, and horse-whipping the true believers. At this the Governor drew near, and as we had often smoked together, and were well acquainted, he saluted me politely, and supposing it to be beyond the reach of possibility that I could venture to do what I was about without a warrant from the pasha, he at once applied himself to cool the rage of the mob. 'You see, my friends', he said, 'that our holy mosque is in a dilapidated state, and no doubt our lord and master Mehemet Ali has sent this Effendi to survey it, in order to its [sic] complete repair. If we are unable to do these things for ourselves, it is right to employ those who can; and such being the will of our lord, the pasha, I require you to disperse and not incur my displeasure by any further interruption.' And turning to me, he said, in the hearing of them all, that if anyone had the hardihood to disturb me in future, he would deal in a summary way with them. I did not, of course, think it necessary to undeceive the worthy Governor; and gravely thanking him, proceeded with my drawing. All went on quietly after this.

During six weeks, I continued to investigate every part of the mosque and its precincts, introducing my astonished companions as necessary assistants in the work of the survey. But when I heard of the near approach of *Ibrahim Pasha*, I thought it was time to take leave of Jerusalem ... '

Thus, Catherwood, with Bonomi and Arundale, made the first complete survey of the Dome of the Rock. After finishing the work, and preparing further drawings for a large panorama of Jerusalem, he returned to London with the intention of writing it up 'in complete and scientific form'. He was unsuccessful in finding a publisher, however, and 'discouraged by the lamentable indifference which he encountered' allowed his drawings to 'slumber quietly in his portfolio'. Bartlett recorded that he treated applications to borrow the drawings 'in a spirit truly liberal and noble', and as a result some were published in works by other authors. All the drawings are now lost, the last record of them being in the autumn of 1846 when James Fergusson recorded that Catherwood handed them over to him for study in connection with his *An Essay on the Ancient Topography of Jerusalem*, 1847, which reproduces two plans and interior view.

Catherwood published a *Description of a View of the City of Jerusalem* with Robert Burford in 1835 which was intended to accompany his panorama, and a *Map of Jerusalem* in Philadelphia in 1846. The Panorama was destroyed by fire in July 1842 in New York, six years after Catherwood first installed it there. The map superseded that of Scoles and was certainly found useful by John Lloyd Stephens who wrote in his *Incidents*: 'I was fortunate to find [in 1836] a lithographic map made by Mr Catherwood ... and which I found a better guide to all the interesting localities than any other I could procure in Jerusalem'.

Lit. V.W. von Hagen, *Frederick Catherwood archt.*, 1950 and *F. Catherwood Architect-Explorer of Two Worlds*, 1968. Information in possession of the writer.

ARUNDALE, Francis Vyvyan Jago (1807-1853)

21 Section of the Dome of the Rock.
Plate opposite p. 104 in J. Fergusson, *An Essay on the Ancient Topography of Jerusalem*, 1847.
Inscribed *Dome of the Rock commonly called the Mosque of Omar. Measured and Drawn by F. Arundale. G. Gladwin, sculp. John Weale 1847.*
Engraving. 27.1 × 18.3.
Victoria and Albert Museum: National Art Library.

22 Jerusalem, From the Mount of Olives.
Plate opposite p. 50 in F.V.J. Arundale, *Illustrations of Jerusalem and Mount Sinai, including the most interesting Sites between Grand Cairo and Beirut*, 1837.
Inscribed with title and *F. Arundale del: L. Haghe zincy. Day & Haghe Lithrs to the King.*
Lithogaph. 29.8 × 23.8.
Victoria and Albert Museum: National Art Library.

Arundale's *Illustrations* provides additional information to supplement Catherwood's account of their drawing and measuring the Dome of the Rock and the Mosque of al-Aqsa. On 28 October 1833 he

DOME OF THE ROCK commonly called THE MOSQUE OF OMAR.

Measured & Drawn by F. Arundale.

21

22

recorded 'I was so fortunate today as to obtain admission into the Court surrounding the Great Mosque, and commenced assisting Mr Catherwood in making measurements of its plan.' On the 5, 6 and 8 December they were again 'measuring the Mosque', and on the 11 Arundale began 'a section of the great mosque which is covered with gilded ornaments. The rock in the centre of the dome still remains and is surrounded by beautiful marble columns. I also began the elevation. The facing of the building is covered with a kind of Dutch tile, which produces a surprising richness of effect ... Mr Catherwood and myself took some heights with the sextant; after which we ascended the dome. This is gained by a bad and very dark staircase. The dome itself is double, there being a space of about three feet between the two shells. The interior is richly gilded. The construction appears extremely good. The windows beneath the dome are double, having tiles on the outside, and painted glass within.'

On the following day they were at the mosque again 'sketching some details for the sections, and also measuring the plan. The diameter of the dome is 66 English feet. One of the sides of the octagon 67 and the Height of the spring 67. This is a remarkably curious coincidence.' In the afternoon Arundale measured the chamber under the rock. After a brief excursion to Bethlehem he returned to the mosque on the 15th, and 'after taking some heights with the

sextant for the section of the dome, I went on with the drawings of the various details: and, among other objects, sketched the box or altar, in which is preserved the print of Mahomet's foot. This no one is permitted to see, though the pious stranger may put his hand into a hole in the wood, and feel, or fancy he feels, the impression; after which he generally strokes his face and beard with the sanctified hand.'

Later, Arundale ascended the staircase and 'attempted to copy the ornament on the dome, but found the task extremely impracticable, from the intricacy of the design. I succeeded however, much better with the ornamented tile work ... and also various patterns on the face of the octagon. By making these drawings I furnished myself with sufficient materials for an accurate elevation or section of this interesting structure to be made on a future occasion.'

Like Catherwood, Arundale handed his drawings over to James Fergusson in 1846 and they are now lost. Two are reproduced in Fergusson's *The Ancient Topography of Jerusalem* (1847), including this elaborate section, the one to which Arundale presumably refers, and which Thomas Hayter Lewis also used 41 years later to illustrate *The Holy Places of Jerusalem* (1888).

Arundale's view of Jerusalem may have been redrawn from one of the pictures he showed at the Royal Academy in 1850 (nos. 1137 and 1191).

BONOMI, Joseph (1796-1878)

23 Diary; covering the period 25 May 1833 to 26 May 1834.
Fifteen small booklets and loose sheets. 11.5 × 18.
Mrs Anthony F.C. de Cosson; widow of Joseph Bonomi's grandson

Joseph Bonomi's diary provides a detailed record of the explorations he, Francis Arundale and Frederick Catherwood, made in the autumn and winter of 1833 in Jerusalem. He describes not only their drawing of the Dome of the Rock, but also their making a panorama of the city. The entries also provide many personal insights not given in the more formal accounts of Catherwood and Arundale, which reveal the hardships and strain of their day to day life. On Wednesday 13 November 1833 for example: 'I had a row with Cath ... his conduct which always appeared ungenerous ... and in some cases unjust ... I have as he says formed so bad an opinion of him that we propose to separate at Beyrout.' This quarrel was still going on two days later: 'I never have passed for these eight years so disagreeable a day as this, perhaps my own doing having told Cath my clear opinion of him we agreed to part immediately which perhaps will be the better plan for it certainly cannot go on so.' But, they did not part, and were soon at work again with their tape measures and pencils. On one evening a few days later, however, when they had used up all their water drinking coffee, Bonomi was 'called to assist poor Arundale [who suffered from epilepsy] no water to pour on his head our usual remedy', and he sent Saleem, his servant, and the 'old man' to fetch water from the river. But, 'they had not been gone long ... when we heard the report of a pistol and Saleem bawling we laid our patient down took our pistols and swords and went towards the stream crying out.' All was well, however, 'Saleem had fired at a wolf or hyena that his fears had made bigger than a donkey.' In the morning 'although Arundale said he was much better while we were helping him on his donkey he fell down in the arms of Cath.' On another morning 'I was woke by an acute pain in my left arm in the fleshy part of the triceps that I soon guessed to be the sting of a scorpion I called up Mr Arundale ... after having tied up the arm immediately at the insertion [of] the deltoid we then scarified a considerable surface the pain being now not confined to one point; I felt relieved after this operation;' but 'my friend now felt unwell himself... .'

ANONYMOUS

24 Perspective view of the Mausoleum of Itimad-ud-daula, near Agra, Uttar Pradesh, India. c.1832.
Pen and water-colour. 83.3 × 55.5.
British Architectural Library: Drawings Collection.

24

The journals of Hodges and William Daniell (nos. 5, 6) make clear that it was not until 1803, when Delhi passed out of the hands of the Marathas and into those of the British, that travellers could move around in the area with any degree of freedom. Naturally, they were fascinated by the architecture they found, and almost immediately began to commission detailed drawings from local Delhi and Agra artists. These artists were not well known established figures, but local craftsmen. Mildred Archer notes that 'there is no documentary evidence to prove in what exact circumstances this painting began but by about 1806 large numbers of drawings which clearly spring from British patronage had been produced. The earliest are on large sheets of Whatman paper with water-marks ranging from 1801 to 1805.' In style and technique they are totally unlike anything produced earlier in India, and their inspiration was probably European architectural drawings. The Indian artists may have seen some of the large volumes of engravings of the classical temples published during the second half of the 18th century, or perhaps the sets of views produced by Italian draughtsmen for sale to Grand Tourists. Alternatively they may have been inspired by the drawings made by the early British civil engineers themselves. Certainly there is an economy of line and treatment which appears to reflect these utilitarian drawings rather than more pretentious topographical views. Until the 1830s when this style of drawing began to be replaced by smaller pictures in which the architecture was given less prominence, many bound sets were taken back to England and survive in various collections.

Lit. M. Archer, *Indian Architecture and the British*, 1968.

JONES, Owen (1809-1874)

25 Unidentified tomb near Cairo perhaps that of the Mamluk Sultan, 'Abd al-Malik. 1833.
Signed with a monogram of the letters OJ.
Pencil and water-colour. Sight size 20.2 × 28.2.
Searight Collection.

This water-colour was used for the illustration on plate IV of *Views on the Nile from Cairo to the Second Cataract. Drawn on stone by George Moore from Sketches taken in 1832 and 1833 by Owen Jones and the late Jules Goury, with historical notices of the Monuments by Samuel Birch*, which was published on 1 June 1843 by Graves and Warmsley. The majority of the plates depict ancient Egyptian architecture, but Jones also included a view by Goury of the interior of the Mosque of Sultan Hasan and three views by himself of other Islamic buildings which were considered by the *Athenaeum* to be 'among the more interesting' plates in the book.

Jones considered the Arabian architecture of Cairo second only to that of the Alhambra. In 1835 he wrote enthusiastically of standing beside the fountain of the Mosque of Sultan Hasan and feeling 'the calm, voluptuous translation of the Koran's doctrines', and in 1856 that the Cairo mosques 'are among the most beautiful buildings in the world. They are remarkable at the same time for the grandeur and simplicity of their general forms, and for the refinement and elegance which the decoration of these forms displays.' It was the study of these buildings which induced Goury and himself to travel north after leaving Cairo to Constantinople, and thence to Granada.

It is worth noting that George Belton Moore (1805-1875) who Jones used to transfer the drawings onto stone had studied under Augustus Pugin with Francis Arundale. He was used by Jones frequently, Jones writing to John Murray in October 1843 that he could 'strongly recommend him as one of the most punctual artists I know'. Later, Moore served with Henry Warren on the Committee of Commissioners for Engraving and Lithography at the Paris Exhibition of 1867.

There are other drawings by Jones and Goury of Egypt, including views in Cairo, in the British Museum and in the Searight Collection.

A note on the back of the present drawing indicates that Professor Creswell considered that the tomb depicted might be that of Qani Bey Emir al-Akhur (Master of the Horse) of 1503-4.

Lit. *Athenaeum*, 24 June 1834, p. 597.
    S. Searight, *op. cit.*, 1969, pl. opposite p. 145.
    R. Searight, *The Middle East*, 1971, no. 42.

JONES, Owen (1808-1874) and GOURY, Jules (1803-1834)

26 Section of the Yeni Valide Camii, Istanbul. 1833.
Stencilled *Ieni Djami Stamboulda* and inscribed with measurements and a scale in metres.
Pencil, pen and ink, and water-colour. 70 × 47.7.
Victoria and Albert Museum (8271C).

25

26

27 Ground plan of the Yeni Valide Camii, Istanbul. 1833.

Stencilled *Ieni Djami Stamboulda* and inscribed with measurements, a key and *Echelle de 0.005 pr metre*. Initialled *OJ*.
Pen and ink, and wash. 50 × 70.4.
Victoria and Albert Museum (8271E).

28 Elevation of a fountain, Istanbul. 1833.

Inscribed with measurements and a scale in metres.
Pencil, pen and ink, and water-colour. 66.6 × 50.
Victoria and Albert Museum (8275).

29 Decoration on the vault of the *türbe* of Süleyman in the cemetery of the Süleymaniye Camii. 1833.

Lettered *Stamboul. La voute du tourbé de Soliman I*, and initialled and dated *OJ Oct 1833*.
Pencil, water-colour and gold paint. 50 × 69.
Victoria and Albert Museum (8273).

30 Decoration on the vault of the Süleymaniye Camii, Istanbul. 1833.

Lettered *Stamboul. Mosquee de Soliman. Rosace de la Grande Coupole* and initialled and dated *OJ Oct 1833*.
Pencil, water-colour and gold paint. 50 × 69.
Victoria and Albert Museum (8272B).

Owen Jones's obituary in the *Builder*, the source for most later writers, states that he went to Sicily and thence 'to Greece, and there met Jules Goury, a French architect, and student like himself ... they went to Turkey, and then to Egypt.' This account is incorrect. Two of the drawings shown here are dated October 1833, and it is known that he and Goury were in Egypt before that. Writing at the time of Jones's death Joseph Bonomi recorded 'I recollect perfectly the arrival of Jones at Thebes. An arab had been sent up to my abode in a tomb, at some little distance from the river, to inform me that two boats had arrived full of Englishmen, and I went down to the Nile in the evening to offer my services. In one of the boats was Owen Jones ... in the other, a French architect M. Jules Goury, and other travellers'. This must have been written before April 1833 when Levinge, the French Consul in Athens wrote to Bonomi 'I suppose ... Mons. Gourie and Jones have left you'.

Nos. 29 and 30 were subsequently used by Jones for the illustrations to plates 37 and 38 for his chapter on Turkish ornament in the *Grammar of Ornament* (1856). Jones considered the architecture and decoration of the buildings of Turkey very deficient in comparison with those of the Arabs. 'We are, however, inclined to believe that the Turks have rarely themselves practised the arts; but that they have rather commanded the execution than been themselves executants ... the decoration of the dome of the tomb of Soliman I at Constantinople ... is the most perfect specimen of Turkish ornament with which we are acquainted.' Unlike the decoration of the Mosque this ornament still survives in its original condition. There is an exterior view of the tomb of Süleyman by Owen Jones in the Victoria and Albert Museum also.

Lit. *Builder*, 9 May 1874, pp. 383-86.
Correspondence in the possession of Mrs L. de Cosson.

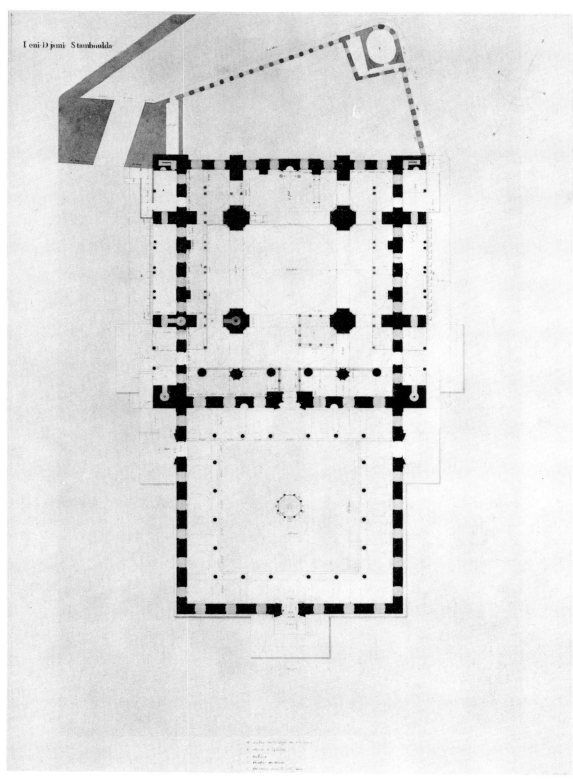

Ieni Djami Stamboulda

27

JONES, Owen (1809-1874) and GOURY, Jules (1803-1834)

31-37 *Plans, Elevations, Sections and Details of the Alhambra,* **1842-45, 1875.**

Returning from France after carrying home the body of his friend Jules Goury, who had died of cholera in Granada on 28 August 1834, Owen Jones determined to publish their drawings of the Alhambra. His decision that the illustrations must be coloured resulted in immediate problems, however, for engraved and hand-coloured plates on the scale he envisaged was impracticable, and no English printer had yet proved himself able to print in colours in the comparatively new art of lithography. Undaunted, Jones decided to be his own printer and publisher, and with help from the

43

29

30

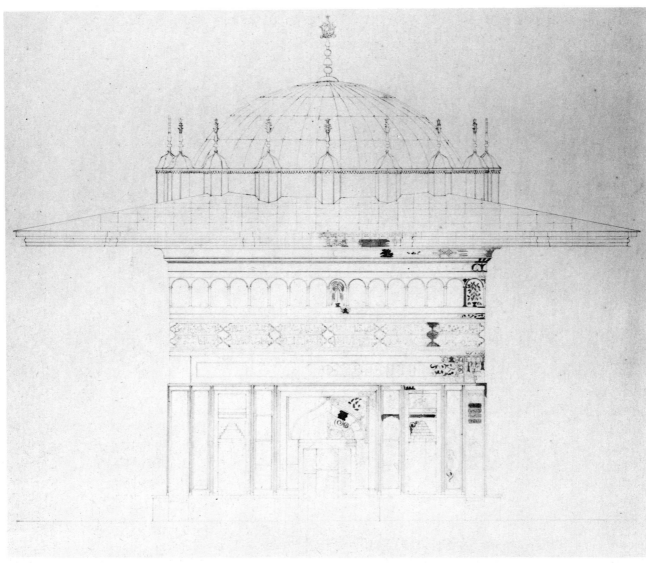

28

firm of Day and Haghe he set up presses at 11 John Street, Adelphi, engaging the 'best ornamental draughtsmen and printers he could secure'. The result was not only the most influential book on Islamic architecture and decoration to appear in this country, but the establishment of colour printing as a new industry.

Plans, Elevations, Sections and Details of the Alhambra: from drawings taken on the spot in 1834 by the late M. Jules Goury and in 1834 and 1837 by Owen Jones, Archt. with a complete translation of the Arabic inscriptions, and an Historical Notice of the Kings of Granada, from the Conquest of that City by the Arabs to the Expulsion of the Moors, by Mr Pasqual de Gayangos was published in two volumes, comprising twelve parts, between 11 April 1836 and December 1845. Volume I, small paper, cost £12 10s, large paper £21, and volume II, small paper £6 6s, and large paper £10 10s. The two volumes, large paper, were offered at £36 10s. Between the production of parts 2 and 3, which appeared together on 15 December 1836, and the

publication of parts 4, 5, 6 and 7 in June 1838, Jones explained in a note to the *Literary Gazette*, that he had been obliged to revisit Spain: 'Mr Owen Jones, in apologising to his subscribers for the delay which has occurred ... has visited Spain, and passed several months at the Alhambra, revising the original drawings, and adding many new subjects; the increased knowledge which might be employed to represent, by lithochromatography, the varied beauties of the Alhambra, having rendered this imperative upon him.' On 8 June 1838 Jones wrote to T.L. Donaldson, the Secretary of the Royal Institute of British Architects, that he had hoped to forward the remaining parts of the volume and the texts for the Institute's library by the end of the year, but delays again ensued, and parts 8 and 9 did not appear until February 1840, and part 10 of volume I, and part I of volume II, in December 1842.

It is difficult to establish with any degree of certainty which plates composed each part. The *Athenaeum* noted on 23 April 1836 that 'it is to be published in numbers each number to contain five

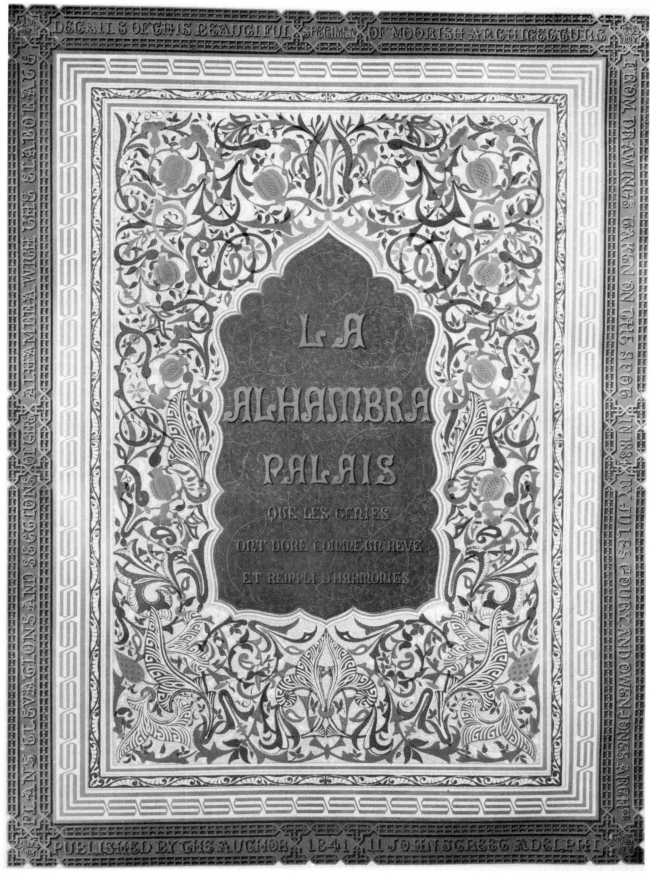

Figure 6

plates, two of which will be Elevations and Sections of the building and the remaining three, Details'. The statement is definite enough for one to suspect that it emanated from Jones, but if so, he must have varied this format slightly, since even excepting the coloured title and end pages, the number of plates is still fifty-one. Furthermore, the implication is that three lithographed and two engraved plates were to appear in each part, but the dates on the plates themselves indicate that this cannot always have been the case. Only three engraved plates, for example, bear the date 1836, yet three parts appeared in that year. The matter is further complicated because details and elevations of totally different aspects of the building appear to have been published together in the same part.

It is also difficult to establish how many copies of the work were printed. Subscribers account for one hundred and sixty-two copies, and a further 64 large paper, 101 colombier and 42 folio, besides 89 'large views of the Court of the Lions', were sold at auction in 1854. Longman, Green and Company took over part of the distribution for Jones in 1848 but retain no records of the number of copies sold. That Jones had intended that more copies than appeared should have been published is certain because '96 copies of letterpress only large paper, 149 copies small paper', and 'a large quantity of surplus letterpress (large and small paper) etc.', was sold by Sotheby, Wilkinson and Hodge in April 1875, as part of his library. The lot, billed as 'the entire remainder with copyright', of 'one of the most sumptuous and valuable works of modern times', also included 288 lithographic stones, 31 copper plates, 23 zinc plates and 26 wood blocks. It was bought for £200 by Bernard Quaritch, the well known publisher and bookseller of Grafton Street, London, who immediately set his presses to work to reprint the two volumes. The result was that in 1877 he was able to advertise in his catalogue as 'now ready, a very carefully prepared issue, in every respect the same as the original edition'. That the existence of this reprint has not been published before now bears testimony to the accuracy of Quaritch's statement.

Lit. M. Darby, *Owen Jones and the Eastern Ideal*, unpublished Ph.D thesis, Reading University, 1974, pp. 42-45, and sources cited therein.

31, 32 Two drawings of tile patterns in the Alhambra. 1833-4.
Lettered *La Alhambra*. 9156m inscribed *Salle des Ambassadeurs ornament G*.
Pencil and water-colour. 9156m 19 × 20.8. 9156n 9.2 × 20.3.
Victoria and Albert Museum (9156m and n).

33 Border designs in the Alhambra. 1833-4.
Pencil, pen and ink, and water-colour. 9156c 16.3 × 13.1. 9156d 17 × 13.2.
Victoria and Albert Museum (9156c and d).

These drawings are among only a handful of those which Jones and Goury made in Spain to have survived.

34 Cast of a detail of the Alhambra taken in 1833, 1834 or 1837.
Plaster.
Victoria and Albert Museum (323-1880).

According to an advertisement for the *Alhambra* dated 25 July 1842: 'to ensure perfect accuracy [of the plates] an impression of every ornament throughout the palace was taken, either in plaster or with unsized paper, the low relief of the ornaments of the Alhambra rendering them peculiarly susceptible to this process; these casts have been of essential service in preparing the drawings for publication, and having been placed with them in the hands of the engravers, have greatly contributed towards the preservation of that peculiar sentiment which pervades the works of the Arabs.'

The casts subsequently passed to the sculptor and modeller Henry Alonzo Smith, as a letter dated 25 March 1880 from James Wild to Sir Philip Cunliffe Owen, Director of the South Kensington Museum, reveals: 'I wish to bring under your consideration the purchase of a few architectural casts which I think worthy of a place in the South Kensington Museum as they might be of great use to students in Oriental Art. They were brought over from Spain by Mr Owen Jones to assist him in the publication of his great work on the Alhambra. The casts belong now to Mr H. Smith of 12 Euston Square – a well known modeller – much employed by Mr Owen Jones ... Mr Smith is now an invalid and as he is about to leave London he wishes to dispose of these casts. The price he asks for them is £5. 5s. 0d.. He also wishes to dispose of upwards of 200 paper impressions or casts from the diaper patterns on the walls of the Alhambra, taken also by Mr Owen Jones. For these paper impressions Mr Smith asks £4. 4s. 0d.. These prices I think are moderate the casts were taken direct from the originals and cannot be procured elsewhere – except by sending to Spain for them.' One cast and the paper impressions were destroyed by the Museum in the present century, but four casts survive of which this is one.

Lit. Victoria and Albert Museum Archives.

35 Paper cover for parts 8 and 9.
Inscribed *'Plans, Elevations and Sections of the Alhambra 'palais que les génies ont doré comme un rêve et rempli d'harmonies'. Victor Hugo. With the Elaborate Details of this Beautiful Specimen of Moorish Architecture: from drawings taken on the spot in the year 1834 by the late M. Jules Goury and Owen Jones, Architects. London Published March 1st 1836, by Owen Jones 11 John St Adelphi, Ackermann & co. 96 Strand, J. Weale High Holborn, and J. Williams Charles St. Soho. Printed in colours by Owen Jones. No. 8 & 9. Price £4.4.0'*.
Lithograph; the part numbers and price added in ink. 50 × 62.7.
Private Collection.

36 The window in the alcove of the Hall of the Two Sisters. Volume I, plate XXI.
Lettered with title in English, French and Spanish.
Chromolithograph. 49 × 68.
Private Collection.

Jones considered that this alcove, with its window overlooking the garden of Lindaraja, was the part of the Palace 'on which the Poets, Painters and

LA ✠ ALHAMBRA ✠

33

Architects of the day bestowed most of their attention. All the varieties of form and colour which adorn the other portions of the palace have here been blended with a most happy effect. Its chief ornaments are the inscriptions which address themselves to the eye of the observer by the beautiful forms of the characters; exercise his intellect by the difficulty of deciphering their curious and complex involutions; and reward his imagination, when read, by the beauty of the sentiments they express, and the music of their composition.'

Jones exhibited a large painting of this subject at the Royal Academy in 1839 (no. 1177).

37 Detail of the ornament in the panels of the Court of the Mosque.
Volume II, plate XVII.
Lettered *no 29 Full size Published by Owen Jones London 1841*
Chromolithograph. 49 × 68.
Private Collection.

PRANGEY, Philibert Joseph Girault de (1804-1893)

38 Interior of the Mosque at Cordoba.
Plate 5 in G. de Prangey, *Monuments Arabes et Moresques de Cordoue, Seville et Granade dessinés et mesurés en 1832 et 1833*, Paris 1836-39.
Inscribed with title in French and *Girault de Prangey del. Villemin lith. Imp de Lemercier, Benard et Cie. Paris chez Veith et Hauser, boul. des Italiens, II*
Lithograph. 56.1 × 40.
Victoria and Albert Museum: National Art Library.

39 Minaret, Mosque of Mohammed el Nager, Cairo.
Plate in G. de Prangey, *Monuments Arabes d'Egypte, de Syrie et d'Asie Mineure dessinés et mesurés de 1842 a 1845*, Paris 1846-55.
Inscribed with title in French and *Girault de Prangey, del 1843. Asselineau lith. Imp. Lemercier a Paris.*
Lithograph. Two sheets joined. 37.5 × 107.9.
Victoria and Albert Museum: National Art Library.

Surprisingly little is known about Girault de Prangey considering that his travels coincided remarkably closely with the other architects and artists whose work is discussed here. He was in Cairo at the same time as James Wild, Edward Lane and others, and in Spain at the same time as David Roberts and John Frederick Lewis. His publications were certainly well known in England. Owen Jones, for example, had copies of both these volumes in his library.

Girault was born at Langres in France and became a student of Fr. Ricois and of J. Coignet. Between 1832 and 1845 he made journeys to Spain and the Near East to make the drawings for the volumes shown here. A third volume entitled *Essai sur l'Architecture des Arabes et des Mors en Espagne, en Sicile et en Barberie*, which was published in Paris in 1841, includes chromolithographed plates depicting the polychromy of the Mosque at Cordova (Plate 4) and the Alhambra (Plate 20). The latter shows the colouring restored in much the same manner as Owen Jones and Jules Goury's *Alhambra*. A fourth volume which Girault published in Paris from 1851, entitled *Monuments et Paysages de l'Orient*, includes prints drawn from topographical views, and suggests that Girault was an accomplished artist as well as architectural draughtsman. The book ceased publication in 1855, however, before all the plates and an 'historical and descriptive text, which he had intended to accompany them, had been published. After completing his travels abroad Girault returned to Langres where he studied the Roman remains there.

37

38

39

40 Details of ornament, Blue Mosque, Tabriz.

Plate 52 in the artist's *Description de l'Arménie, La Perse et La Mésopotamie*, volume 1, Paris 1842.
Lettered with title and *Ch. Texier del. H. Roux aine lith. Chromolith, Engelmann et Graf, Paris.*
Chromolithograph. Size of page 32.5 × 50.
Victoria and Albert Museum: National Art Library.

41 Elevation and part section of the Masjid-i Shah, Isfahan.

Plate 78 in the above volume.
Photograph.

Texier's volume includes a number of chromolithographs of Islamic ornament amongst numerous black and white plates depicting classical and other buildings, and reinforces the point made in the introduction to this section, that polychromy was one of the outstanding features of the Near Eastern experience for architects brought up in the neo-classical tradition.

This volume was not, in fact, the first of Texier's publications to include drawings of Muslim buildings. His first, and equally important work, the three volume *Description de l'Asie Mineure* (Paris, 1839-49), also contains elaborately detailed plans and elevation of mosques and other architecture, some of which, 'La Mosquée Verte, Nicée' (now known as the Yesil Cami at Isnik), for example, are also coloured. These volumes were the result of three journeys which Texier undertook on behalf of the French government between 1833 and 1837, during which he determined numerous sites and ancient cities previously unknown. On the first he discovered Pessinunte, which was 'the key to the geography of Asia Minor', and on the second, which took him to the southern coast, he explored the ruined cities of Lycia and Pamphylia. On his third journey, which commenced in 1836, he crossed the peninsula from Tarsus to Trebizond, following the course of the Euphrates, and on his return to Constantinople was decorated by the Sultan with the order of Nishan Iftikar, 'in recognition of his services in aid of geographical science'.

The two volumes titled *L'Arménie, la Perse et la Mésopotamie*, of which the first is shown here, were the result of a fourth journey which Texier made between 1839 and 1841 in company with the Comte de la Guiche and Comte Jaubert. On this occasion he crossed Armenia, Mesopotamia and Persia, and returned through Babylon, Syria and Egypt.

Texier was well known in this country and his work was so much admired that in 1864 he was awarded the Royal Gold Medal of the Royal Institute of British Architects. He always deemed this to be the greatest honour which he ever received, and reciprocated by presenting to the Institute no less than thirty-three large portfolios containing the series of original measured sketches and finished drawings he had made on his travels. In the following year he published with Richard Popplewell Pullan *The Principal Ruins of Asia Minor* (1865), but this does not include any drawings of Islamic architecture.

40

41

Texier's volumes undoubtedly had some influence here, both Owen Jones and William Burges, for example, are known to have had copies in their libraries.

Lit. *Builder*, 8 July 1871, p. 522.
G. Vapereau, *Dictionnaire Universel des Contemporains*, 1858, p. 1651.

WILD, James William (1814-1892)

42 Two sketch books open at pages depicting ornament on buildings in Cairo.
Pencil, pen and ink, and water-colour. Page size 12.6 × 17.6.
Victoria and Albert Museum (E.3842, 3843-1938).

43 View of Cairo looking towards the Mosque of Sultan Hasan. c.1842.
Inscribed with title.
Pencil and water-colour. 31.2 × 20.8.
Victoria and Albert Museum (E.3832-1938).

44 The Mosque of Sultan Hasan, Cairo. c.1842.
Inscribed with title and *details see book to* . The gaps are left blank.
Pencil and water-colour. 31.1 × 26.
Victoria and Albert Museum (E.3833-1938).

45 Interior of the house occupied by the artist J.F. Lewis, Cairo. 1842.
Inscribed *Section of the Mandarah, Mr Lewis House in Cairo*.
Pencil, pen and ink, and water-colour. 43.8 × 31.1.
Victoria and Albert Museum (E.3763-1938).

James Wild was one of the most serious students of the Islamic architecture of Cairo in the first half of the last century, but is little known by modern historians. He began his architectural career with several small gothic churches, and followed these in 1840 by his most famous work, Christ Church at Streatham, in which he was assisted by Owen Jones (see nos. 49-51). It was perhaps through his friendship with Jones, who in 1842 married his sister Isabella, and with Matthew Digby Wyatt, both of whom he had probably first met at the meetings of the Architectural Society, that Wild first became interested in Near Eastern studies, and was motivated to join Joseph Bonomi on Lepsius's great expedition to Egypt in 1842. During the course of the expedition he contributed a number of letters to the *Athenaeum*, in one of which he explained for the first time what is now currently accepted as the method by which the pyramids were built.

After the termination of Lepsius's expedition, Wild stayed on in Cairo, where the writer of his obituary in the *Builder* recorded that 'he studied deeply the mosques and domestic architecture of the Arabs, on which he was considered a good authority. In his investigations he adopted the native dress, in order to penetrate the mosques.' This description was further elaborated by C. Purdon Clarke in the *Journal of the Royal Institute of British Architects*: 'it was a curious trait in his character that he never was an antiquary, nor cared for the great mass of those connected with the edifices he devoted so much time to study ... he cared more for dwellings of Burgher people than for temples and palaces, and as these houses were selected for careful study on their merits rather than their history in his sketch books an invaluable record has been preserved of domestic interiors, especially of Cairo and Damascus.' The many hundreds of meticulous drawings made by Wild now in the Victoria and Albert Museum (presented by his daughter Elizabeth Wild in 1938), and the drawings he made while a member of Lepsius's expedition now in the Griffith Institute, Oxford, testify to the accuracy of Purdon Clarke's observation.

Several further interior views and a ground plan of the house of the painter John Frederick Lewis, who lived in Cairo for ten years from 1841, are also preserved among Wild's drawings in the Victoria and Albert Museum.

Lit. *Journal of the Royal Institute of British Architects*, 30 March 1893, pp. 275-6.
Builder, 12 November 1892, p. 384.
Athenaeum, 25 February 1843, pp. 189-90.

LEWIS, John Frederick (1805-1876)

46 Recess in a chamber of the painter's house in Cairo. 1841-50.
Inscribed *Mendurah in my house at Cairo* and signed *J.F. Lewis*.
Pencil and water-colour. 54.9 × 38.2.
Victoria and Albert Museum (717-1877, E.5679-1910).

This view of the same mendurah as drawn by James Wild (no. 45), serves to point up the difference between the artistic and architectural conceptions of Islamic architecture in the early 19th century. Lewis undoubtedly drew what he saw, his pencil emphasising every imperfection to convey a sense of the present as part of the past, the mendurah as witness to centuries of oriental passion and intrigue. Wild's drawing is set in a different period, the wooden screens are depicted as new; his desire to understand and record their structure leaves no room for literal or romantic interpretation.

Lewis lived in Cairo for almost ten years from 1841, his house apparently being one of the oldest and most picturesque in the city. Thackeray visited him there in 1844, writing in his *Notes of a Journey from Cornhill to Grand Cairo* (1846): 'we made for J's quarters; and in the first place entered a broad covered court or porch; where a swarthy tawny attendant, dressed in blue, with white turban, keeps a perpetual watch [then] we came into a broad open court, with a covered gallery running along one side of it. A camel was reclining on the grass there; near him was a gazelle to glad J. with his dark blue eye; and a numerous brood of hens and chickens, who furnish his liberal table. On the opposite side of the covered gallery rose up the walls of his long, queer, many windowed, many galleried house ... the paint was peeling off the rickety, old, carved galleries; the arabesques over the windows were chipped and worn; — the ancientness of the place rendered it doubly picturesque ... Hence we passed into a large apartment, where there was a fountain; and another domestic made his appearance ... this fellow was clad in blue too, with a red sash and a grey beard. He conducted me into a great hall, where there was a great, large, Saracenic oriel window ... all the ceiling

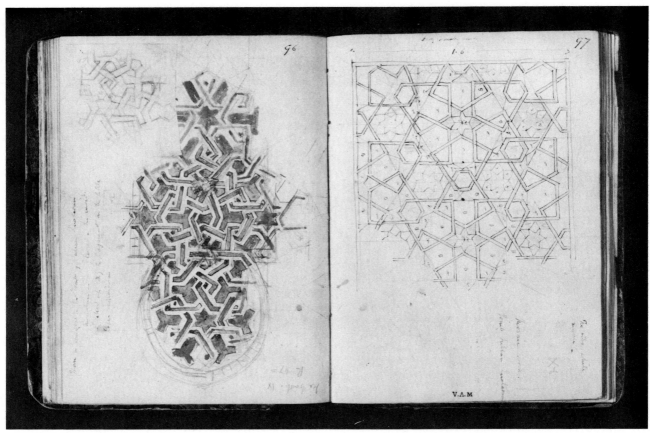

42

43

44

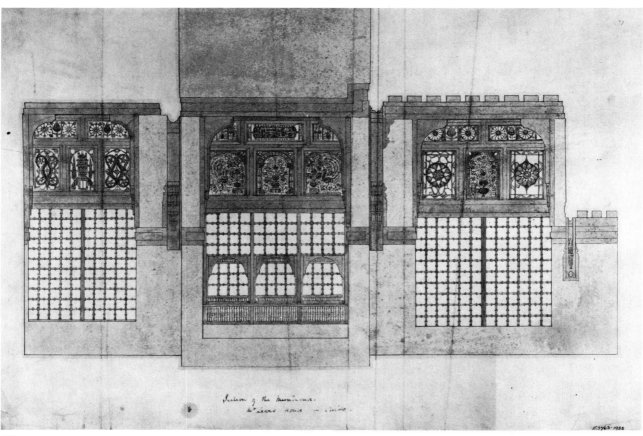

45

46

is carved, gilt, painted and embroidered with arabesques, and choice sentences of Eastern writing. Some Mameluke Aga, or Bey, whom Mehemet Ali invited to breakfast and massacred was the proprietor of this mansion; it has grown dingier, but, perhaps, handsomer, since his time. Opposite the divan is a great bay window, with a divan likewise around the niche. It looks out upon a garden ... A great palm-tree springs up in the midst, with plentiful shrubberies and a talking fountain ... ' And so Thackeray's long description continues, and all the time there was a pair of 'the most beautiful, enormous ogling, black eyes in the world' looking down through the holes in a screen.

Lit. *John Frederick Lewis RA. 1805-1876*, Laing Art Gallery, Newcastle, 1971.

ALLOM, Thomas (1804-1874)

47 Interior of a Turkish caffinet, Constantinople.
Inscribed with title, and signed and dated *T. Allom July 7 1838*.
Water-colour. 30.1 × 23.
Searight Collection

Thomas Allom was trained as an architect in the office of Francis Godwin and worked on many important public and private buildings with him before leaving to devote himself to painting. He spent a considerable time touring on the continent and in the Near East to produce the illustrations for many topographical books published by Fisher, Son

and Company, Virtue and Company, and Heath and Company. These plates, like the work of his contemporary W.H. Bartlett, assisted in the popularisation of Islamic architecture in the early 19th century. Allom's drawings, according to his obituary in the *Builder*, were 'eagerly sought after not only in this country but in many continental cities.'

Coffee drinking was an important part of daily life in the Near East, and buildings were set aside especially for this purpose. Richard Pococke, *Description of the East* (1743), explains that 'The coffee houses ... are remarkably pleasant; many of them are large rooms, and the cieling [sic] of them are supported with rows of pillars, round which they have their sopha's; there is generally a court behind them with a basin of water, and a fountain in the middle ... in these coffee houses they have concerts of musick at certain hours every day; and in some, a person paid by the house tells at a fix'd hour Arabian stories in a very graceful manner, and with much eloquence. These coffee houses answer the end of publick houses with those, who openly drink nothing but water, coffee, and sherbets; where all idle people, strangers, and others, who are not of the first rank, pass their leisure hours, send to the shops for their provisions, and take their repasts.'

This drawing was engraved by W.H. Capone for Fisher's *Illustrations of Constantinople and Its environs or Constantinople and the Scenery of the Seven Churches of Asia Minor*; 'illustrated in a series of drawings from Nature by Thomas Allom

47

with an Historical Account of Constantinople and Descriptions of the Plates by the Rev. Robert Walsh' (1828), where it appears opposite page 59 in volume I.

Lit. *Builder*, 26 October 1872, p. 840.
   Information from R. Searight.

BARTLETT, William Henry (1809-1854)

48 A street, the Shâri'a el-Gohergîyeh, in Cairo, with the Mosque of Ibn Kaláûn, the Medreseh and tomb of Mohammed-en-Nasir, and the Barkûkîyeh.
Water-colour. 30.5 × 42.4.
Victoria and Albert Museum (D.13-1903).

Although, strictly speaking, Bartlett falls into the category of topographical artist, he was trained as an architect, and no account of the study of Islamic architecture in the early 19th century would be complete without mention of him. Indeed, Beattie, one of his patrons and author of several of the volumes which Bartlett illustrated, considered that his work showed evidence of a concern for accuracy which distinguished it from that of other artists. It was 'devoid of mannerism ... Bartlett's subjects are drawn with admirable accuracy of line and ... Original in style and colouring, they faithfully portray both the architecture and the landscape of every individual scene, and are not deteriorated by imitation of any popular or fashionable artist.' Although the contemporary historian might not agree with Beattie, the work of other artists in the

Near East clearly eclipsing Bartlett's work in both finish and detail, it is certainly true that Bartlett was without equal in the range and number of subjects he depicted.

Awareness of the appearance of the Near East for the great majority of the British public in the first half of the 19th century undoubtedly came about through knowledge of the illustrations which Bartlett provided for a series of popular travel books written by himself, and other authors including *Walks about the City and Environs of Jerusalem* (1844); *Views Illustrating the Topography of Jerusalem Ancient and Modern* (1845); *Forty Days in the Desert* (1848); *The Nile Boat* (1849); *Gleanings, Pictorial and Antiquarian on the Overland Route*, (1850); *In the Footsteps of Our Lord and His Apostles in Syria, Greece and Italy* (1851); and *Jerusalem Revisited* (1854), many of which ran through several editions. These were prepared during six visits Bartlett made to the Near East in 1834-5, 1837, 1842, 1845, 1853 and 1854. Not surprisingly he encountered many of the architects featured in this section of the exhibition, and their exploits occasionally provided him with material for his books; see, for example, no. 19 'Mr Catherwood's Adventure'.

Lit. Notice by John Britton, *Art Journal*, 1855, pp. 24-26; reprinted privately in the same year.
   W. Beattie, *Brief Memoir of William Henry Bartlett*, 1855.
   P. Ferriday, 'A Victorian Journeyman Artist', *Country Life*, 15 February 1968, pp. 348-9.

48

SECTION 3

OWEN JONES AND HIS CIRCLE

Part 1
Islamic architecture and a 'new style'

Argument about which style of architecture and decoration was best fitted to express the aspirations of the Victorian age raged during the middle of the 19th century. The Gothic and Renaissance schools dominated the field and have been much studied as a result. Rather less well known is the school that believed in a 'new' style. It was to this movement that the Islamic enthusiasts, and in particular Owen Jones, belonged.

In 1835, while preparing his *Alhambra* for publication, Jones gave a lecture to the newly formed Architectural Society entitled 'On the Influence of Religion upon Art', in which he made clear what course of development he felt architecture should take in the future. Colour as he had experienced it in Islamic buildings was obviously to play a major part, but now he attempted to show how a form capable of taking colour could be evolved from the products of modern technology. The main thesis of Jones's argument was that great works of architecture were the products of religious inspiration, and that as the power of religious conviction declined, so did artistic creativity. But, he pointed out, 'the Reformation have [sic] destroyed Religious architecture, and the chain which held society linked together'. On its ruins had arisen a religion more powerful 'whose works equal, nay, surpass all that the Egyptians, Greeks, or Romans had ever conceived [but not the Mohammedans!] Mammon is the God; Industry and Commerce are the high-priests. Void of poesy, of feeling, or of faith, they have abandoned Art for her bolder sister Science.'[1]

Thus, science was to be the guiding force in modern architecture, and the use of new materials made available by modern industry would in themselves result in the creation of a new and appropriate style. Nowhere, however, does he state how the structural and the aesthetic were to be combined, or what response the new architecture was intended to provoke, leaving his listeners to assume that it would be similar to feeling 'the calm voluptuous translation of the Koran's doctrines' in 'the fairy palace of the Alhambra'.

In attempting to create this new architecture in the 1840s Jones readily used new materials but in giving them expression drew too literally on his Eastern sources, and was misunderstood by his contemporaries as a result. A design he submitted in competition for St. George's Hall, Liverpool, in 1839 was noticed by one reviewer on account of its 'singularity; the exterior is a specimen of Italian architecture of some merit; in the interior, the rich decorations, the painted roof, and the slender columns, shew that the architect seems to have been imbued with a love for his favourite Alhambra. The building, however, is much too fantastic for execution;'[2] and by another reviewer, as 'in a sort of Alhambra fashion, but after such fashion as to give us what is offensive in it, without what renders it charming.'[3]

When, a few years later, Jones entered a design for the Army and Navy Club, the *Athenaeum* remarked that 'three or four designs pronounced their own rejection at once on account of the singularly inappropriate style adopted. Among these ... is one in the Alhambra style by Mr Owen Jones',[4] and the *Builder* noticed, 'Mr Owen Jones has not been able to forget the Alhambra, his design being throughout a clever attempt to reproduce that style'.[5] In 1849 another design for a villa for Alderman Moon, which Jones showed at the Architectural Exhibition, was noticed by the same periodical as 'founded on the Alhambra, clever but as it seems to us unsuitable;'[6] while another commentator noted that the 'pretensions to design consist only of a flowering over the walls with a sort of Alhambra pattern.'[7]

Some idea of the appearance of these abortive schemes can be gathered from two houses which Jones did build, at numbers 8 and 24 Kensington Palace Gardens (nos. 53-56). Although his attempt to give his Moorish designs a sense of structural necessity is successful in the balcony supports of no. 24, the same accusations which had been made of Alderman Moon's villa seem applicable to no. 8. Indeed, Blashfield himself apparently did not altogether approve of the Moorish details and remarked to the Commissioners for Woods and Forests 'the Moresque ornament of the windows might be removed ... with a stroke of the pencil the design would then be strictly Italian and as *I wish*.'[8]

Jones was clearly aware of these strictures, and in order to add validity to his use of the Moorish style, exhibited at the Royal Academy from 1835 a series of large, elaborately coloured, and minutely detailed drawings of the Alhambra, all of which are now lost. Two of these, exhibited in 1839 and 1840, created a considerable stir. The *Civil Engineer and Architect's Journal* considered that the first reduced all the other interiors to a secondary rank,[9] and the *Athenaeum* described it as 'one of the most magnificent displays of gorgeous colour and elaborate tracing we ever saw.'[10] It was, in fact, the only architectural drawing which the *Athenaeum* noticed, and marks the date from which regular reviews of the architectural room commenced in that periodical.

· The production of such large and elaborate drawings was unusual in England at the time. While Jones knew at first hand the work of French and German architects which he had seen on the continent, his immediate inspiration may have been the exhibition of Zanth's drawings at the Institute of British Architects in 1838. These excited much favourable comment because of their size, complexity and degree of finish, and like Jones, Zanth used gold leaf in place of gold paint. Zanth's visit was occasioned by his need to gather information for the Moorish Villa Wilhelma (no. 52) which he was designing for the King of Württemberg, and it seems likely that he met Jones at this time.

While Jones grappled with the problem of re-creating an Islamic experience in a form which was acceptable to his contemporaries, James William Wild, his future brother-in-law, and Joseph Bonomi, his close friend, conceived other answers to the problem which also made use of their Eastern experiences. Working primarily from the form and structure of Near Eastern buildings, as opposed to their decoration, Wild designed Christ Church at Streatham (nos. 49-51) which immediately brought praise from the critics and remains quite the most successful of the works in the 'new style'. Bonomi's Marshall's Mill at Leeds, a commission he received through the painter David Roberts in 1842, is excluded from this study because the design was based on ancient Egyptian prototypes.[11]

More successful than his architectural designs of the 1830s and 40s were those Jones prepared for books and tiles. Several reviewers of the *Alhambra* remarked particularly about the intricacy of Moorish patterns, and Jones's explanation of their derivation from a series of geometrical grids. Jones realised that understanding such designs lay at the heart of rationalising the building's fantastic qualities, a fact which César Daly also acknowledged, concluding his long review of the *Alhambra* in the *Revue Générale de l'Architecture*, which he edited, 'rien n'est plus simple, et cette méthode fournira une nouvelle preuve de la vérité que nous n'avons cessé de répéter depuis la publication du premier numero de cette *Revue*, à savoir: qu'il faut allier la science à l'art, si l'on veut être un grand artiste, et que la géométrie est la base de toutes les études de forme.'[12] Nowhere was this

debt to geometry more obvious than in the mosaic dadoes which surrounded the lower portions of the walls of several of the halls. Jones admitted to being fascinated by the 'great variety in their patterns', and by the infinite possibilities for the 'invention of designs',[13] and it is consequently not surprising that he should have interested himself in contemporary developments in mosaics and tiles on his return (nos. 58-61). That these were new materials produced by modern scientific processes, and that geometry was 'la base de toutes les études de forme', made their study in the context of the 'new style' particularly appropriate.

Like tile design, page design is confined to two dimensions, but whereas the former is restricted to geometrical patterns, no such limitations existed in the latter. Thus, Jones was able to explore, at will, the possibilities of the adaptation and combination of Moorish designs with ornament from other sources. Initially, as in the designs for J.G. Lockhart's *Ancient Spanish Ballads* (1841) (no. 63), he made little effort to integrate these eclectic borrowings in single patterns but seems to have been content to allow their individual images to form a mental unity. Later having been exposed to Indian and Persian manuscripts, he was able to produce *Paradise and the Peri* (1860) (nos. 79-80) with wholly integrated designs. In most of his work of the 1840s and 50s, however, his involvement with Gothic manuscripts, which he collected, and with naturalism, which he increasingly came to see as the true inspiration for design, eventually asserts itself, to the exclusion of recognisably Moorish forms.

In the early 1850s Jones's involvement with the Department of Practical Art and with the decoration of the Crystal Palace caused him to adopt a radically new approach to Islamic ornament which is detailed in the next section. This new concern, with the principles adopted by the Muslim artists rather than with the specific forms of their ornament, and with the possibilities of iron and glass, resulted in his designing a series of buildings which fulfilled all that he hoped a 'new style' might achieve. While some, the crystal palaces at Muswell Hill and St. Cloud, and his design for the Manchester Art Treasures Exhibition building, for example, came to nothing, the St. James's Hall, the Crystal Palace Bazaar, and Osler's shop were built, and were greeted enthusiastically by his contemporaries. Christopher Dresser's description: 'And when, in St. James's Hall, we appear to be transplanted to some fairer world — art is here! ... the beauty is excessive, and thereby the spirit is rendered glad, and is entranced by harmonies; the proportions of the parts are just, the enrichments beautiful, and the colours glorious and fair; the whole is display of knowledge, and learning, and judgement', could just as well have been applied to the Alhambra.

Seen in relationship to the work of his contemporaries, even those prepared to use large amounts of iron, like Sydney Smirke in the British Museum Reading Room (1852), or James Bunning in the Coal Exchange (1847), Jones's designs were quite extraordinary and almost incomprehensible without prior knowledge of his peculiar, Islamic rationale. But although Jones's designs were consistent within themselves, in the wider spectrum of 19th century architectural development, engineering forms and polychrome patterns did not make architecture, as the *Builder's* obituary of Paxton made abundantly clear, by denigrating his work on the Crystal Palace. Not all buildings could be hidden behind existing façades so that they required no external detailing, nor could they be constructed entirely of iron and glass.

Thus, when Jones entered the competitions for the National Gallery (1867) and the St. Pancras Hotel (1865), both buildings which necessitated elaborate displays of traditional materials and plastic forms, his designs failed to impress, and the shortcomings of his work, as fitted for conventional architecture, were revealed. Consequently, the story of his career in the last fifteen years of his life is largely one of an increasing concern with decorative work, the interiors for Alfred Morrison (nos. 85, 36), for example; and with pattern designing such as the silks for Warners (nos. 74-75) and the wallpapers for Trumble, and Jackson and Graham (nos. 72, 73).

Notes

1 A copy of this lecture, privately printed by Jones's friends in 1863, is in the Victoria and Albert Museum: National Art Library.
2 *Gentleman's Magazine*, CLXVIII, 1840, p. 69.
3 *Civil Engineer and Architect's Journal*, 1840, p. 188.
4 *Athenaeum*, 8 May 1847, p. 497.
5 *Builder*, 8 May 1847, p. 214.
6 *Builder*, 10 March 1849, p. 109.
7 *Civil Engineer and Architect's Journal*, April 1849, p. 99.
8 Letter dated 11 October 1843 in the files of the Crown Estate Office.
9 *Civil Engineer and Architect's Journal*, June 1839, p. 216.
10 *Athenaeum*, 1 June 1839, p. 418.
11 Correspondence concerning the Mill is in the possession of Mrs de Cosson.
12 *Revue Générale de l'Architecture*, VI, 1845, p. 52. It would seem that Jones lent Daly the wood blocks used for the small illustrations in the *Alhambra*, for this article.
13 *Alhambra*, letterpress to plates XL and XLII.

The West Front.

E.3647-1938

49

WILD, James William (1814-1892)

49 Design for the west front of Christchurch, Streatham. 1841.
Inscribed *The West Front*. Signed with a monogram of the letters JW and dated *1841*.
Pen and ink and water-colour. 25 × 18.5.
Victoria and Albert Museum (E.3647-1938).

50, 51 Modern photographs of the exterior, and the interior showing the decorations by Owen Jones on the apse ceiling.
National Monuments Record.

Critics of Christ Church have had great difficulty in deciding exactly which style is represented, descriptions ranging from 'Romanesque of the South of Europe', to 'Lombardic' and 'Byzantine'. James Wild's skill in blending his eclectic, particularly Islamic, sources so as to disguise their origin and to produce a unified design was much commented upon by his contemporaries. The *Builder*, for example, described it as 'unrivalled in its excellence as a modern basilica'.

The first suggestion that a church should be built at Streatham was made in the late 1820s, when the Reverend Henry Blunt put in hand the process of raising funds. By the late 1830s some £6,340 had been acquired and Wild was recommended by the Bishop of Winchester who praised his 'powers of design, originality, and accuracy of estimates'. The foundation stone was laid on 11 August 1840, although Wild's initial designs were not approved until 8 December. Building was completed by 19 November 1841, when Christ Church was dedicated. Three early sketches for the front façade are in the Victoria and Albert Museum, of which no. 49 is one. The general form and arrangement is Italian Romanesque, like Lewis Vulliamy's church of All Saints, Ennismore Gardens, which had been designed in the previous year, although not erected until later, but the detailing is clearly Islamic with cusped and horseshoe arches, and striped brickwork. These sketches formed the basis for Wild's contract drawings which were completed by 9 April 1840. After construction had commenced in August, he revised the design, forwarding new drawings for the front and side elevations which are dimensioned about five feet above the ground thus indicating the state of work at that time. The new designs considerably tighten the composition and further emphasise its Eastern aspects. The earlier Italianate cornice has been substituted by an Egyptian cavetto one – Wild ruled out Byzantine as being 'rather pretty than noble'; the tower has been altered to include trelliswork and lesenes, recalling the Giralda at Seville; a clerestory has been added; and the main west door, framed by an arch like that of the Mosque of Sultan Hasan in Cairo, has been allowed to assume a greater importance. Wild, however, was still not content with the design, and when in 1842 the *British Almanack* illustrated a study, apparently based on a further drawing in the Victoria and Albert Museum, for the main front he added a 'carved and painted tympanum', designed by Joseph Bonomi, above the west door. Later still, this and the clerestory were omitted, and two pylons were added flanking the entrance.

At the time of dedication the interior had been left undecorated through lack of funds. Wild obviously intended that it should be decorated since a drawing of two bays depicting red and white voussoirs is preserved in the Victoria and Albert Museum, and the contract drawings show coloured Islamic chevrons, stars and capitals. Owen Jones later provided new designs which appear to have been completed by November 1851, when Henry Cole recorded being taken by him to see them. The apse ceiling and capitals are all that now survive of Jones's scheme.

Wild's previous church designs had been sensitive and competent renderings of the accepted Gothic and Norman styles, although Coates Church at Whittlesey, Cambridgeshire, with its central nave, lean-to aisles and detached tower, was similar in plan and massing to Christchurch. His reason for adopting what he considered to be essentially a 'Byzantine' style at Streatham was, he claimed, one of expense. The funds provided were not sufficient 'for carrying into effect a uniform design founded on any models belonging to our English Gothic'. He aimed, instead, for 'quiet severity', and borrowed freely from other sources to achieve this. But the question remains of where these sources came from, because, of course, Wild did not visit the East until after the design for Christ Church was completed, and he was only twenty-four years old when it was begun. The answer must be that they came from Owen Jones and Joseph Bonomi. Before the completion of the church, directories record that Wild was living at Jones's address, and Jones could certainly have provided all the information and drawings he needed. The interior bay elevation, for example, described as deriving from the 'Great Mosque at Constantinople', could easily have been taken from drawings by Jones like that exhibited here (no. 26).

Lit. M. Darby, *op. cit.*, 1974, pp. 177-181, and sources cited therein.
Victorian Church Art, Victoria and Albert Museum Exhibition catalogue, 1971, p. 66. (No. G10illus).

ZANTH, Karl Ludwig Wilhelm von (1796-1857)

52 Interior view of the Villa Wilhelma, Cannstadt, near Stuttgart. 1855.
Plate in K.L.W. von Zanth, *La Wilhelma: Villa Mauresque de sa Majesté le Roi Guillaume de Wurtemberg*, Paris 1855. Lettered *L. de Zanth, inv. etdel.. Kellerhoven, Lith..*
Chromolithograph. Size of page 63 × 48.
Victoria and Albert Museum: National Art Library.

King Wilhelm I of Württemberg (1781-1864), being 'desirous to form for himself a kind of special personal retreat or suburban villa, to which he might occasionally retire for the day or a few hours', commissioned Zanth to prepare designs, and formalised this in a proclamation dated 6 April 1837. The villa was to stand below Rosenstein, his palace on the banks of the River Neckar at Cannstadt, near Stuttgart. On the 16 July Zanth wrote to a friend in Paris that the project was to embrace a 'théâtre d'été' and a 'pavillon de bains dans le style Mauresque accompagné de serres au

50

51

52

milieu d'un parc'. In the following year Zanth visited England to examine hot houses, fountains, and their machinery, especially at Chatsworth. It seems extremely likely that he also saw Owen Jones at this time. Zanth's friend T.L. Donaldson, who arranged an exhibition of his work at the Institute of British Architects during his visit, which was much praised in architectural circles and must have been seen by Jones, does record in his *Memoir* of Zanth that 'the volume of Owen Jones was the only authentic reference' for the Moorish style of the villa. Furthermore, King Wilhelm was a subscriber to the *Alhambra* and it is possible may have been influenced in his choice of style by the reception of the first parts of Jones's work. It should also be remembered that Jones must have been known to Zanth through their mutual friend Jacob Ignaz Hittorff.

The théâtre d'été was inaugrated on 29 May 1840; a casino, which grew out of the project for a 'pavillon de bains', was begun in the spring of 1842; and an extensive complex of garden pavilions added in the summer of the same year. The casino was eventually opened on 30 September 1846 when

it was used for the wedding celebrations of the Prince of Württemberg who married the Grand Duchess Olga of Russia on that day, and the gardens were finally completed by 21 October 1851, when they were opened. The Villa has now been incorporated into Stuttgart zoo.

Although Zanth may have turned to Jones's work for specific details, neither the *Alhambra*, nor any other architectural publication apparently inspired the Villa Wilhelma's Moorish style. The King's decision was based, as Zanth explains in the introduction to his book, primarily on literary sources: 'l'idée qu'on attache ordinairement à l'architecture mauresque repose en générale sur les récits des Orientaux.' At the same time, however, he does refer to the 'Mosque' in the gardens of the Royal villa at Schwetzingen, near Mannheim, built by Nikolaus von Pigage, 1778-1795, which is similar in plan to the Wilhelma. Zanth himself claimed to follow 'Greek' rather than Moorish principles in the design, and it is certainly very difficult to detect particular sources in his work

Some drawings for the Villa Wilhelma survive in the Hittorff archive, Wallraf-Richartz Museum, Cologne.

Lit. D. van Zanten, *op. cit.*, Chapter IV, part II.
    T.L. Donaldson, 'Memoir of Louis de Zanth', Royal Institute of British Architects *Papers*, 16 November 1857, pp. 15-18.

53

JONES, Owen (1809-1874)

53-57 Nos. 8 and 24 Kensington Palace Gardens, 1843 and 1845.

In June 1838 the Treasury appointed a Committee to enquire into the management of the Royal gardens. As a result it was decided to improve land at Frogmore using funds realised from letting the kitchen garden adjacent to Kensington Palace on building leases, and James Pennethorne and Thomas Chawner, as architects to the Commissioners for Woods and Forests, the forerunners of the present Crown Estate Office, drew up plans. These allowed for a road to be constructed from what is now Kensington High Street to Bayswater, to be called the Queen's Road – its name was quickly changed to Kensington Palace Gardens – and the provision of thirty-three plots in all. The plots were to be let on ninety-nine year leases from 1842, and the new houses were to be provided with ornamental gardens and boundary walls, and to be finished ready for habitation within two years.

Twenty applications were received but all were rejected as unsuitable. In July 1842 Samuel Strickland, a speculator, was successful in acquiring five, and erected moderately sized villas which he quickly sold. The rents and restrictions

imposed by the Commissioners on the remaining plots, however, deterred others until July 1844 when John Marriott Blashfield signed an undertaking to build twenty-one houses of a cost at not less than £63,000 within five years. At the time of embarking on this venture Blashfield appears to have had no previous experience of property development. The reluctance on the part of established architects and builders to accept the Commissioners terms may have warned him of possible pitfalls, but does not appear to have affected his initial enthusiasm. Given the resources of Wyatt and Parker, the building firm for which he worked, he probably assumed that he could not go wrong. Within two years, however, he was in serious financial difficulties having spent £60,500 on the erection of five houses not one of which had sold. His debts included a mortgage of £42,000 on which he did not pay the interest repayments, and a security of £10,000 in part purchase of Wyatt and Parker's business. Even so, he wrote to the Commissioners that he had the 'fullest confidence' in the ultimate success of the venture. By April 1847, however, he was in further difficulty, and finally, on 14 May, he was declared bankrupt. Responsibility for completing the work fell to the assignees of his estate amongst whom was Thomas Hayter Lewis. In August 1847 they offered the whole property for sale but received no bids, and finally, towards the close of 1849, handed back the unsold plots to the unwilling Commissioners, who were obliged to complete the work themselves. Blashfield is estimated to have lost £40,000, but this did not prevent him from emerging a few years later as an important and successful terra cotta manufacturer.

One cannot help surmising that Blashfield's downfall may have been the result of his involvement with Owen Jones. Jones not only assisted with his colour printing, but also designed various architectural enrichments for him including mosaics, vases, balustrades, etc.. Although these appear in Blashfield's catalogues after 1847 some were incorporated in houses before that date, and it seems likely that Jones produced designs through Blashfield for Wyatt and Parker too. The precise terms of their arrangement over the development of Kensington Palace Gardens are not known. Jones was certainly involved with part of the administrative responsibility because his name appears on two broadsheets inviting applications for leases, and it was to Jones that Blashfield turned for two of the designs. It seems likely in view of Blashfield's lack of experience in similar schemes, and of Jones's involvement at so early a date, that Jones may have been responsible for advising him to undertake the project in the first instance. Jones's first house cost five times more than it need have done, and was much larger than the Commissioners had envisaged. To a certain extent it set the pattern for the remainder of the road, of palaces rather than houses, and of expense and unsuitability which was what led to Blashfield's downfall. The scheme has a sense of scale and grandeur which is reminiscent of some of Jones's later projects, and was surely not part of Blashfield's original intention.

Lit. M. Darby, *op. cit.*, 1974, pp. 162-75, and sources cited therein.
G.L.C. Survey of London, XXXVII, *Northern Kensington*, 1973; pp. 151-64, 183-4.

53 8 Kensington Palace Gardens, c.1845.
Lettered *Garden Front of villa no. 3 Queen's Road, Kensington Palace Gardens Owen Jones Archt.*
Lithograph. 40.6 × 29.1.
Kensington Reference Library (K61/951).

54 Design for part of the drawing room ceiling, 8 Kensington Palace Gardens. 1843.
Water-colour. Octagonal 47 × 47.
Victoria and Albert Museum (8352).

55 8 Kensington Palace Gardens shortly before demolition in 1961.
Photographs.
Kensington Reference Library.

Within days of making his offer to the Commissioners Blashfield forwarded plans, elevations and details, prepared by Owen Jones, for a villa on plot 6, later numbered 3 and then 8. Although at first glance these adhered to the popular Italianate paradigm, the façades were richly encrusted with cement ornamentation in a Moorish style, and the balcony walls and parapets pierced with fretwork designs. On 13 October Pennethorne reported that the house was larger than the Commissioners had expected, and had two entrances instead of one, 'as regards the elevations. We have to observe that from the general forms, and the richness of the ornament the design will probably produce an appearance equal to that originally intended for this site and we do not feel that we ought to object to the peculiarity of the proposed Moresque enrichments though hitherto not much adopted in this country, but we think Mr Blashfield may be obliged to reconsider the details (and to substitute others more classical [deleted]).' About Jones's plan for the entrance gates, lamps and pallisading, they commented that it had 'been designed in the Moresque style ... we understand that Mr Blashfield wishes to apply it to all the plots let to him ... the design submitted cannot fail to produce a rich effect though (its regular irregularities [deleted]) not altogether in accordance with hitherto approved models.' In the event this design for the railings was not carried out.

Although the house was probably finished by December 1845 when Henry Cole recorded having been to see it, another seven years passed before it was occupied, the purchaser being a Mrs Caroline Murray who paid Blashfield's mortgagees £6,300, less than half the £15,000 required to build it. Mrs Murray immediately applied to convert the house into two flats claiming that the reason that it had remained empty for so long was because it was too large. The Commissioners agreed, and the architects F. and H. Francis undertook the work. Subsequently, many other alterations were carried out by later owners. These included the enlargement of the conservatory, by J.W. Fraser in 1885: 'this room I propose to extend in length for the placing of my large organ, the whole will be carried out in the spirit of the existing Alhambric decorations.'

By 1952 the house was empty and reported to be 'dilapidated'. The Crown Estate Office showed some determination to save it but the structure proved unsafe and it was demolished in 1961.

The lithograph of the garden façade is based on a water-colour which Jones showed at the Royal Academy in 1845 (no. 1235); and it was probably this picture which he also showed at the International Exhibition, 1862.

Lit. J. Physick and M. Darby, 'Marble Halls', *catalogue of the Exhibition of Architectural Drawings*, Victoria and Albert Museum, 1973, pp. 79-80.
M. Darby, *op. cit.*, 1974, pp. 163-73.

56 24 Kensington Palace Gardens.
Modern photograph courtesy of G.L.C..

On 26 August 1845, a little over a year after submitting his plans for no. 8 to the Commissioners, Blashfield forwarded another design by Owen Jones for a villa on plot 19, later numbered 24. Pennethorne reported 'the house will be large, handsome and well disposed, I see no reason for objecting to either the plans or elevation although the latter is in a Moresque style, which (though not usually adopted) is admired by some persons and produces a picturesque effect.' Building began in

54

October, and two months later was sufficiently advanced for Blashfield to apply for the lease. This was granted on 23 December, and on the following day mortgaged by Blashfield to Lewis Vulliamy for an undisclosed sum. Delays in building then ensued, for by May 1847 the property was not completed although work was well 'advanced', with the exterior 'finished down to the cornice above the ground floor windows'. Vulliamy applied to the Commissioners for an extension of their original agreement with Blashfield until the middle of the following year, and this was granted on 16 July 1847. Within one month, however, he sold the house to James Ponsford, a builder, who completed the work and took up residence in the house with his wife and family in 1849. Although Blashfield had

spent over £9,000 on the property it was sold at the auction of his estate for only £3,400.

Many alterations were made by later owners including the removal of 'cement ornaments' on the front façade in 1879, and the building of a large gallery on the back for the then owner, Chester Beatty, in 1934, before the property passed to the present lessee, the Government of Saudi Arabia.

Jones's designs for the house have not survived so that it is difficult to know exactly what he originally intended. The overall form is again Italianate, but based more on the palazzo than the villa, the details, however, as one would expect, have no Italian precedents. The balustrades and interlaced mouldings of the second floor window surrounds appear to derive from Turkish or Cairene sources,

55

56

but the huge spreading naturalistic patterns of the brackets which carry the first floor balcony, although undeniably Moorish, have no precedents and seem to reflect Jones's awareness of earlier criticism of his 'Moorish' designs that they were nothing more than a 'flowering over the walls with a sort of Alhambra pattern'.

Lit. M.Darby, *op.cit.*, 1974, pp. 173-175.
    G.L.C. Survey of London, XXXVII, *Northern Kensington*, 1973, pp. 183-84.

ANONYMOUS

57 Panel from the sanctuary of St. Mary's Church, Rhyl, designed by John Hungerford Pollen (1820-1902) in 1863, and demolished in 1976.
Plaster, painted. 31.7 × 53.8.
Peter Howell.

It is not clear how this panel, which appears to be identical with those incorporated into the walls of no. 8 Kensington Palace Gardens by Owen Jones, came to be used at St. Mary's, Rhyl. Hungerford Pollen was a considerable authority on ornamental art, and a member of the teaching staff at South Kensington from 1864 to 1877, and it is possible that he may have acquired it as a suitable accompaniment for his Celtic and Byzantine ornament in the church.

Plaster was naturally one of the materials in which Jones took a particular interest. He had made minute studies of the elaborate plaster ceilings of the Alhambra, and experimented with various methods of reproducing them after his return to England. Of particular importance, both in the context of his work of the 1850s and 60s, and for architecture in general, was his involvement with the Frenchman Leonarde Alexandre Desachy over the development of fibrous plaster. William Millar in *Plastering Plain and Decorative* (1897), the standard work, believed that Desachy, who had taken out a patent in 1856 for 'producing architectural mouldings, ornaments, and other works of art formed with surfaces of plaster' – what was subsequently called fibrous plaster – had first obtained the idea for it from 'Reinaud, Prisse d'Avennes, Girault de Prangey or others who had very fully described and illustrated Egyptian arts and architecture.' In fact, it seems much more likely that Owen Jones or Joseph Bonomi may have provided the inspiration.

Jones almost certainly met Desachy in Paris when he and Matthew Digby Wyatt were arranging for casts to be taken of various antiquities in the Louvre for display at the Crystal Palace at Sydenham. Desachy carried out this work and immediately came to London to assist at Sydenham, where he was chiefly employed with Bonomi in building the Aboo Simbel figures from plaster, wood and linen on a brick core. Both Bonomi and Jones had had some experience of making casts themselves, and it seems likely that the ideas for the wider use of plaster may have evolved at this time. However that may be, it was Desachy who patented the material, and who, in advertisements, called himself 'the inventor of patent canvas plaster casting'.

Some time shortly after 1860 Desachy returned to France and left the business to J. McDonald and R. Hanwell, his foreman and chief modeller. At this time Millar states that he was 'pecuniarly indebted' to Jones, although he does not say why. This debt, however, apparently handicapped the efforts of McDonald and Hanwell to keep the business running profitably to such an extent that in 1863 they gave up, and it was taken over by G. Jackson and Son.

Lit. A. Pollen, *John Hungerford Pollen*, 1912, pls. 19A, 19B.

JONES, Owen (1809-1874)

58-61 Designs for tiles.

Jones admitted to being fascinated by the great variety of tile patterns in the Alhambra, and by the infinite possibilities for the 'invention of designs'. It is not surprising therefore that he should have interested himself in contemporary developments in mosaics and tiles on his return from Spain in 1834. Apart from his printing work it was, in fact, as a designer of tiles and mosaics that he was probably best known during the 1840s.

Speaking in 1858, Matthew Digby Wyatt noticed that experiments in the manufacture of three types of tile – encaustic, azulejos, and mosaics – had been undertaken earlier in the century. Herbert Minton had attempted to manufacture encaustic tiles as early as 1828 but had experienced technical difficulties, largely stemming from the different expansion and contraction rates of the constituent clays. Although he was able to tender for floors in 1836 and 1837, it was not until the early 1840s, when he made the tiles for the Temple Church, that he perfected their manufacture with any degree of success. While Minton was conducting these experiments, John Marriott Blashfield, Jones's collaborator over the development of Kensington Palace Gardens, was carrying out his own experiments in making mosaic and tessellated pavements, and in 1839 was able to lay an elaborate floor for Thomas Hope at his villa, Deepdene.

Owen Jones became much involved with these experiments after Blashfield applied to Minton for a supply of tesserae made by a new process patented on 17 June 1840 by Richard Prosser, an inventive manufacturer from Birmingham. Although conceived by Prosser as a means of making buttons, Blashfield realised its applicability to the manufacture of mosaics and tiles, and persuaded Minton to set up two machines for this purpose. Tesserae made in this way proved very successful and encouraged Blashfield, who was a subscriber to Jones's *Alhambra*, to employ him to prepare a series of ten designs showing their use in different patterns. Later, Blashfield also employed Matthew Digby Wyatt to copy mosaics in Italy, and it was a selection of these drawings which were subsequently published by Wyatt under the title *The Geometrical Mosaics of the Middle Ages* (1848).

The third type of tile mentioned by Wyatt were azulejos. These, he recorded, were also made by Minton, who ascertained the process of manufacture after 'careful study of some fragments brought to this country by Mr Owen Jones (from Spain) and of those which form the well known pavement of the Mayor's chapel at Bristol.' The patterns on these tiles were painted or printed on a white slip covering the earthenware body. Since many, in illustration, look similar to the tessellated and encaustic varieties, it is difficult to be certain which are which. They were certainly used by Jones in the Alhambra Court at Sydenham (no. 96). Wyatt also recorded that 'various modifications of azulejos, some perforated and others modelled into foliage were introduced at the suggestion of the late Welby Pugin,' though he does not state where they were used. Another modification, involving printing on the tile lithographically, may have been suggested by Jones too.

By the end of the 1850s other firms had also entered the market: John Henry Maw who bought up Chamberlains and employed Jones and Wyatt to produce designs; Wyatt and Parker who advertised 'tessellated pavements and encaustic or inlaid ornamental tiles' as early as 1842, some of which were also designed by Jones; and Godwin of Lugwardine, to name but three. These developments reflected a vast increase in the use of tiles and mosaics in secular and ecclesiastical buildings which lasted until the turn of the century.

Jones's most important tile design, for the floors of the Houses of Parliament, is now lost. Described as 'Moorish' by commentators at the time it was submitted in competition in 1843, and very favourably received when exhibited to the public in April 1844, it has been stated that it was partly carried out. There is no documentary evidence to support this, however, the floors as they exist are known to have been made by Minton, and appear to be straightforward designs by Barry and Pugin.

58 Title page, J.M. Blashfield, *Designs for Mosaic and Tessellated Pavements by Owen Jones Archt.,* **1842.**

Lettered *Design for Mosaic Pavements by Owen Jones Archt. 1842. Printed in colors by Owen Jones 9 Argyll Place. Published for the proprietor by J. Weale, High Holborn, London 1842.*

Chromolithograph. 25.1 × 34.8.
Victoria and Albert Museum: National Art Library.

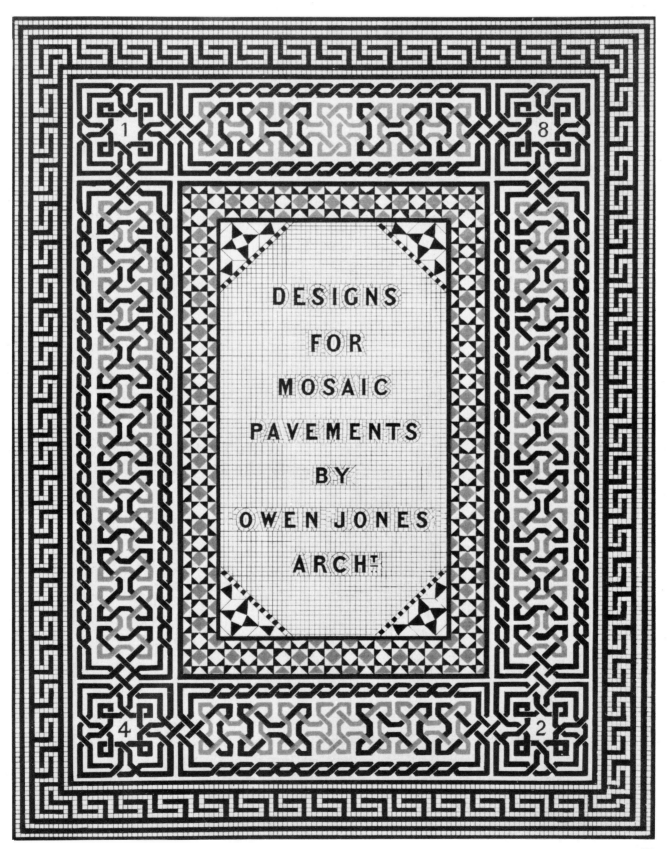

**59 Mosaic tesserae probably made by Mintons.
c.1845-50.**
Private collection.

60 Design for a tile pattern. c.1855.
Lithograph and water-colour. 30.2 × 35.
Victoria and Albert Museum (8115.12).

59

60

61 Designs (10) for tile patterns. c.1855.
Lithograph and water-colour. Each hexagonal 10 × 11.6.
Victoria and Albert Museum (8115.5).

Blashfield was so impressed by the ten designs which Jones prepared for him in 1842, that he employed Jones to print them, and they were published by John Weale as *Designs for Mosaics and Tessellated Pavements by Owen Jones Archt.*.

This volume, and the ingenuity of the process, aroused considerable interest, and on 11 March 1843, three days after Blashfield had demonstrated a press and shown designs at the Society of Arts, he also exhibited them at a *soirée* held by the Marquess of Northampton, as President of the British Association. There they were noticed by, amongst many others, the Prince Consort, who requested an account of the process to be written for him. This

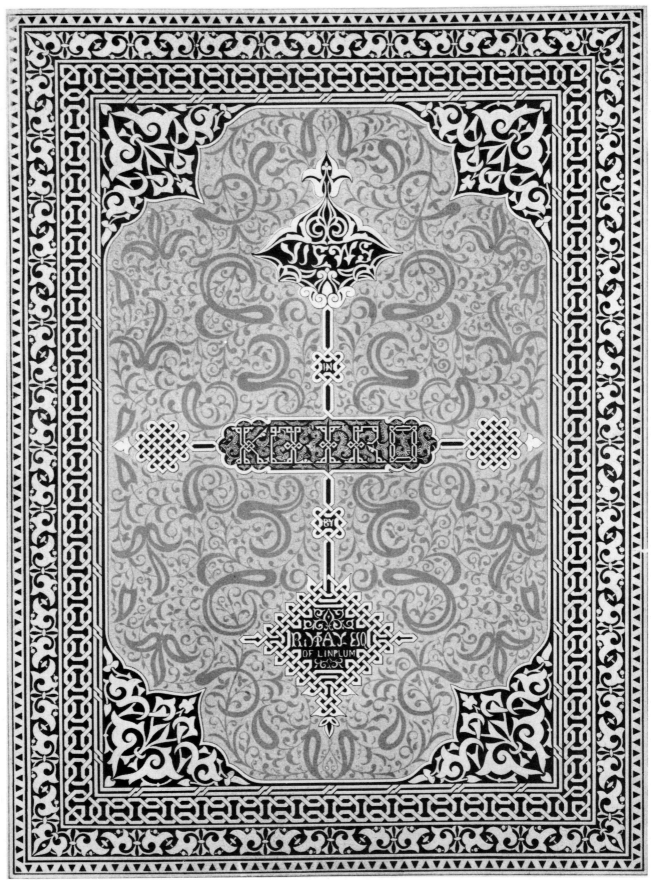

62

was prepared by Frederick Oldfield Ward, a friend of Jones and Bonomi, and presented to the Prince four days later. At the same time Blashfield arranged for this material to be included in a second edition of Jones's *Designs*, and put in hand the publication of another work entitled *Encaustic Tiles*, 'with ninety-six copies of antient tiles drawn half the full size, and also designs of pavements. The drawings ... arranged and copied on stone by Mr Owen Jones'.

In the plates of the book of *Designs* Jones begins with a series of simple borders adapted from Pompeian ornament into which he introduces red bands interlacing with black, 'a feature of the Moresque mosaics', and progresses through adaptations of Greek fragments, seen in the Museum at Naples, to elaborate Moorish interlacing patterns formed from polygonal, triangular and other shapes. In a series of designs now in the Victoria and Albert Museum, which are apparently much later in date, and were worked out on a prepared grid, Jones's borrowed motifs are no longer recognisable, yet in the rhythmic insistency of the patterns and the evocative, hot colours, his Islamic experience is still clearly discernible.

Lit. M. Digby Wyatt *On the Influence exercised on Ceramic Manufactures by the late Mr Herbert Minton*, 1858.
J. Barnard, *Victorian Ceramic Tiles*, 1972.
M. Darby, *op. cit.*, 1974, pp. 114-121.

JONES, Owen (1809-1874)

62-64 Early Books.

Even before the *Alhambra* had finished being published Jones was using his presses for other work, and he continued to do so until the early 1850s when his expanding architectural practice would no longer permit it. During this time he became involved with various publishers including John Murray, Longman, Green and Longman, and Day and Son, and as a result, his work as designer, printer, or writer, is to be found in at least fifty volumes published between 1840 and 1870. If one adds to this the work of Jacob Wrey Mould, Henry Warren and his son Albert Henry, Charles Aubert, E.L. Bateman and others, who either assisted Jones or were his apprentices, the number can be doubled.

As has already been noticed, Jones's production of his *Alhambra* marks the advent of colour printing as an industry in this country; with the numerous other books and plates he now produced, Jones could also be said to have founded the market for the 'illuminated' as opposed to 'illustrated' gift book. The designs in very few of these volumes are without some trace of Islamic influence, even those depicting flowers or naturalistic subjects, or those based on Gothic illuminated manuscripts of which Jones was particularly fond, include interlacing parallel lines, scrolls or other features which can be traced back to an origin in Islamic decoration.

Lit. R. McLean, *Victorian Book design*, 1972.
M. Darby, *op. cit.*, 1974, pp. 123-47.

62 Title page to Robert Hay, *Views in Cairo*, 1840.
Chromolithograph. 36.6 × 50.
Victoria and Albert Museum: National Art Library.

The story of the production of this volume is told under no. 16. This title page which was designed and printed by Jones was one of the first commissions he took on having set up his presses to produce the *Alhambra*. The only other plates he is known to have produced, which pre-date this, apart from those in the *Alhambra* are those in J.G. Wilkinson, *The Manners and Customs of the Ancient Egyptians*, published from 1836.

63 Title page and opening in J.G. Lockhart, *Ancient Spanish Ballads*, 1841.
Chromolithograph, wood block and letterpress. Size of page 20 × 24.6.
Private Collection.

Jones's first work for the publisher John Murray, a new illustrated edition of Lockhart's *Ancient Spanish Ballads*, which had first appeared in 1823, was to prove one of the most important and influential books which he designed. Work on the *Ballads* was sufficiently advanced by November 1839 for Jones to send Murray 'a proof of the key plate and some on which I have dabbed a little water-colour which does not of course pretend to show the effect they will have when printed but simply the arrangement', and by December he was at work upon a stone 'like Old Mortality to immortalise us both', and 'getting on in earnest'. Early in 1840 Jones reported that he had looked the book over with Henry Warren 'with reference to borders, etc.' and Murray advertised that the volume would be ready in January 1841. Delays ensued, however, for in February of that year Jones sent him a proof of one of the borders, and asked 'have the proofs of Warren's blocks turned up yet?' In the event the book was published on 16 October 1841, at two guineas in a gold blocked cover, or at £2. 12s. 6d. in Morocco. Besides the designs by Warren, the *Ballads* also includes illustrations after William Allen, David Roberts, William Simpson, C.E. Aubrey, William Harvey, S. Williams and Louis Haghe.

Jones's work involved not only the design and printing of five title pages, but also the design of coloured borders and vignettes, printed from wood blocks by the Vizetelly brothers who were also responsible for printing the text. John Murray had originally entrusted the letterpress to James Vizetelly, their father, but during the production of the *Ballads* his enterprise collapsed. The combination of their economical colour printing in single tints, with Jones's chromolithography, established the *Ballads* as the first example of a new form of literature. Contemporary critics noticed its appearance with considerable enthusiasm and their commentaries presaged a new era in publishing history in which a general revival of interest in book ornamentation was to become apparent: 'the illustrations of this splendid volume ... are carried throughout with a luxury hitherto unexampled in

63

63

this country', 'so beautifully embellished volume was never offered to the world', 'exquisite'.

Jones's illustrations in the *Ballads* are not confined to adaptations of Moorish ornament alone, many derive directly from Gothic architectural forms and others are copied from nature. The different styles of these ornaments, their relationship with the line drawings of the other artists, and their sometimes awkward juxtaposition with the text, combine to render the book visually disturbing for the modern reader. Six years after it was published Jones wrote to Murray: 'It is very difficult in a few papers to judge of the effect of a book as a whole, when completed it should be seen in the 'mind's eye'.' The mental image left by the *Ballads* apparently satisfied Jones, the combination of abstracted eclecticism, and of text and illustration, producing an academic unity. Certainly it appealed to the public, for a second edition was needed in 1842 and a third, in which Jones introduced a number of new designs, was published in 1856.

64 Prayers and Thanksgivings, opening in *The Book of Common Prayer*, **edition published by John Murray, 1845.**
Chromolithograph. 16 × 23.7.
Private Collection.

Following the success of the *Ballads* Jones prepared a number of other books for John Murray including a new edition of *The Book of Common Prayer*

published in 1845. The formula was much the same as that for the *Ballads* with text, wood cut illustrations, initials and borders by the Vizetelly brothers, and title-pages lithographed by Jones himself. For the most part the printing is in red and black, but the Communion Service is printed with added blue, and the Psalms with added orange. The relationship of the text and illustrations is much more carefully controlled than in the *Ballads*, and confined rigidly, with the exception of the titles, within' a regular framework of one or two single lines. When combined with the relatively larger space left for the margins this has the effect of tightening the composition and appearance of the volume considerably. Fragmentation is less obvious, and it is no longer easy to prescribe particular models for Jones's ornament, the individual components of which, like the Gothic and Islamic elements in this plate, are more subtly mixed.

Besides engravings after Raphael, Overbeck, Angelo de Fiesole, Poussin and Fra Bartolomeo, the volume also includes illustrations by J.C. Horsley and Henry Warren, and 'historical subjects carefully drawn from the originals, by George Scharf Jun. under the superintendence of Lewis Gruner'.

64

HARVEY, William (1796-1866)

65 Illustration in E. Lane, *The Thousand and One Nights, commonly called, in England, The Arabian Nights' Entertainments,* **volume 1, 1841.**
Wood engraving. Size of page 15.1 × 23.8.
Victoria and Albert Museum: National Art Library.

Harvey was undoubtedly the most prolific of the wood engravers working in an Islamic style. Like Henry Warren, he apparently never visited the East and relied instead on the publications and advice of those who had. In the case of the several hundred illustrations he provided for Edward Lane's translation of the *1001 Arabian Nights*, published by Charles Knight between 1838 and 1840, Harvey not only used the volume of drawings by Coste which Hay had lent to Lane (no. 15), but also drawings by Lane himself, to assist him with the details. It was no doubt the success of this book, and Northcote's *Fables* (1828-33), Harvey's best known work, which encouraged John Murray and Owen Jones to commission him to carry out the Moorish illustrations for J.G. Lockhart's *Ancient Spanish Ballads* (1841) (no. 63).

Lane subsequently used both the drawings he had done himself in Cairo and those by Coste, in preparing the illustrations for his *Modern Egyptians*, first published in 1837.

Lit. E. Lane, *Modern Egyptians*, 1837, Preface.

MOULD, Jacob Wrey (1825-1886)

66 Bandstand, Central Park, New York, 1859-1886.

Original photograph. 32.5 × 23.8.
British Architectural Library (LS 3322/5).

Mould was Jones's most talented pupil and took to New York, where he moved after finishing his apprenticeship, his master's ability to combine vigorous eclectic designs with bright polychromy. In 1892 Montgomery Schuyler described him as 'the most successful colorist in Architecture whom we have ever seen in New York', and a review of Mould's scheme for the decoration of a house belonging to John Gray of 1859, described him as not having served under Jones 'in vain', and as 'bold as a lion in the selection of his colors, and grave as a judge in their combination, he dazzles with brightness, without offending the most fastidious taste; and as to design, we must pronounce it exquisite ... every line and every leaf betrays the spirit and life of a master hand, and reminds us of the best works of the Alhambra and Gartner's modern production in Munich.'

In his work for the New York Parks Department, in which he co-operated with F.L. Olmsted and Calvert Vaux, he was called upon to design 'everything from guard's badges and telegraph poles to a large casino using iron, stone, wood, tile, glass, papier mâché and combinations of them all'. The bandstand, now demolished, was particularly prominent, distinguished by its bright polychromy. From the base upwards the colours included: 'olive green; red-brown moulding; broad band of yellow with red and black ornamental ... leaf forms; narrow black line; narrow red line; moulding in sky blue; ogee moulding in pea green,' and so on, to the roof where the colours were 'within and without ... far brighter'. Mould's extravagant compositions, like those of Jones's himself, rarely succeed in disguising a fundamental debt to Islamic ornament. Forms identifiable as Moorish appear in many of his works, sometimes assertively as here in this bandstand, but more frequently combined with naturalistic designs, as in the stonecarving of the balustrades to the terrace steps in Central Park, or with strong Italian Gothic polychromy, as in the voussoirs of the Metropolitan Museum, or the black and white banding of All Souls' Unitarian Church – the Church of the Holy Zebra – New York.

Lit. D. van Zanten, 'Jacob Wrey Mould: Echoes of Owen Jones and the High Victorian Styles in New York 1853-1865', *Journal of the Society of Architectural Historians*, XXVIII, pp. 41-57.
Information in the possession of the writer.

PHILLIPS, Henry Wyndham (1820-1868)

67 Portrait of Owen Jones. 1856.

Oil on canvas. 84 × 126.
British Architectural Library: Drawings Collection.

The success of the Crystal Palace, and the publication of the *Grammar of Ornament* (1856), established Owen Jones's reputation on an international level. On 22 July 1857 he was awarded the order of St Maurice and St Lazarus by the King of the Italians; and on 23 September in the same year he received, through his acquaintance with Sylvain van der Weyer, the Belgian Ambassador to London, the Order of King Leopold of the Belgians. At the same time, Jones's friend Prosper Merimée recommended him to the French Government for the Legion of Honour, but political wrangling prevented the award from being bestowed. In England, Jones's labours were recognised by the Royal Institute of British Architects which commissioned this portrait, and which awarded to him the Royal Gold Medal in March 1867.

Henry Wyndham Phillips, the son of Thomas Phillips a well-known portrait painter, also painted other travellers to the east including J.H. Drummond Hay 'in a Moorish costume', exhibited at the Royal Academy in 1838 (652); J.G. Wilkinson, exhibited 1842 (138); and A.H. Layard, exhibited 1848 (652). Between 1845 and 1849 he exhibited scriptural subjects at the British Institution, and like Owen Jones's pupil Albert Warren, he was a keen member of the Artists' Rifles.

Lit. P. Merimée, *Correspondence Générale*, XVI, 383-4.
  Art Journal, 1869, p. 29.
  Athenaeum, 1868 (ii), p. 802.

JONES, Owen (1809-1874)

68 Osler's Gallery, Oxford Street, London. 1858-60.

Pen and ink, and water-colour. 102 × 147.3.
Victoria and Albert Museum (P.29-1976).

Following his work for the Departments of Practical Art, and Science and Art, and for Paxton at the Crystal Palace at Sydenham, Jones designed three extraordinary London interiors which utilised his new understanding of 'principles', and achieved an Islamic splendour in their effect. The St. James's Concert Hall off Piccadilly opened 25 March 1858; the Crystal Palace Bazaar, on the corner of Oxford Street and Lower Regent Street, in December 1858; and Osler's gallery, in Oxford Street, in June 1859. All have now been demolished.

Osler's, the famous Victorian glass manufacturers, had been founded by Thomas Osler and a Mr Shakespeare in Birmingham in 1807. Their business had rapidly expanded, and in 1845 they were able to take a thirteen year lease on premises at 44 Oxford Street to act as a London showroom. In 1847 the firm completed a standing candelabrum, some sixteen feet high, for Ibrahim Pasha which was much admired by all who saw it, including Prince Albert, and this led to a series of commissions for similar objects many of which decorated palaces abroad, particularly in India, where the firm also opened a showroom. Jones's first involvement with Oslers appears to have taken place in 1850 when they were making arrangements to site their crystal fountain in the centre of the Great Exhibition and were considering asking Charles Barry to make the design for it. Later, when the fountain was moved to Sydenham, Jones was undoubtedly involved with the firm again. The commission to design the Oxford Street gallery came in 1858 when the lease on number 44 expired, and the firm acquired number 45, the neighbouring site, with permisson to demolish the existing buildings and to erect new ones.

Like the St. James's Hall and the Crystal Palace Bazaar, Osler's Gallery involved the use of coloured glass, fibrous plaster, iron and other new materials. The main area of the shop consisted of a display gallery 106 feet long 24 feet wide and 25 feet 4 inches high which was entered through a vestibule paved with Minton's polychrome tiles in geometric shapes. Longitudinally the roof of the gallery was divided into fourteen compartments containing stained glass in geometric panels of fibrous plaster, while along the walls, and at one end, were a series of large mirrors, which being placed opposite one another produced an effect of extended space. Jones's drawing depicts more than fourteen bays, and it is not clear whether he deliberately exaggerated the length for picturesque reasons, or whether this represents an early design which was not carried out.

The impresssion created by the repetition of the reflection of so many small areas of bright colour from numerous facets of cut glass resulted in a 'fairy-like' effect which caused the gallery to be classed as one of the 'sights' of London. In 1862 Jones added a wing to the north east which the *Art Journal* described as surpassing the principal gallery in its 'intrinsic beauty of effect'. The gallery was demolished in 1926.

Like the St James's Hall and Crystal Palace Bazaar, Osler's Gallery was an attempt to make permanent the effects which Jones had succeeded in achieving in the Great Exhibition. The three buildings derived their structural form and component materials from the Crystal Palace but their decorative finish from Jones's work of the 1840s. The iron shell was there, but Jones placed no emphasis on it, preferring instead to hide it with plaster, and it was this material moulded into various patterns to make the framework for stained glass and mirrors that emphasised the space in three dimensions and most clearly echoed the framework of the Crystal Palace. Thus, the linking of light and colour was more explicit and more tangible because the space was clearly defined by the surfaces which composed it; a vitreous effect was achieved, however, with the stained glass and the mirrors, and it was these, coupled with the pendant gas burners and primary colours, which gave the building its ethereal, eastern aspect.

Lit. J. Physick and M. Darby, *op. cit.*, p. 102.
  M. Darby and D. van Zanten, 'Owen Jones's Iron and Glass Designs of the 1850s', *Architectura Zeitschrift für Geschichte der Baukunst*, I, 1974, pp. 60-1.
  M. Darby, *op. cit.*, 1974, pp. 369-388.

67

MESSRS J AND C OSLERS GALLERY 45 OXFORD STREET
OWEN JONES ARCHITECT

68

Figure 7

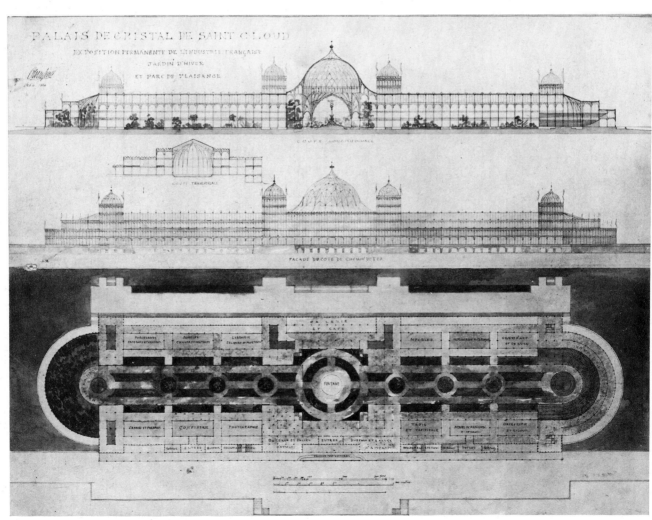

JONES, Owen (1809-1874)

69 Plan, elevation and sections of an iron and glass building designed for a site at St Cloud, Paris. 1860.

Inscribed *Palais de Cristal de Saint Cloud, Exposition Permanente de l'Industrie Française. Jardin d'Hiver et Parc de Plaisance. Coupe Longitudinale. Façade du Côté de Chemin de Fer. Coupe Transversale* and with scales in feet and metres.
The plan is inscribed with titles of different areas. Signed and dated *Owen Jones Oct 4 1860.*
Pen and ink, and water-colour. 63 × 48.2.
Victoria and Albert Museum (E.10-1937).

The culmination of Jones's ferro-vitreous designs in his 'new style' was a series of projects for colossal exhibition buildings none of which was carried out. This particular drawing was based on an earlier proposal for an almost identical building which Jones designed for the site on Muswell Hill now occupied by 'Alexandra Palace' (fig. 7). The Great Northern Palace Company was formed in 1858 with the intention of providing an institution for the population of north London like that which the Crystal Palace at Sydenham did for that in the south. Working with Sir Charles Fox, the engineer, Jones produced 18 drawings and a plaster model for the new company by December 1858. These are now lost, but their appearance can be judged not only from the St Cloud drawing, but from contemporary descriptions which appeared at the time of their exhibition at the St James's Hall and elsewhere.

The most prominent feature of Jones's design was a large, circular dome 200 feet in diameter springing from a masonry foundation 36 feet above the ground level. This was enclosed by four towers connected by galleries and flanked by naves, each of which terminated in two further towers and semi-circular colonnades. A further semi-circular protrusion in the centre of the north façade, omitted in the St Cloud design, accommodated a lecture theatre providing seats for 10,000 people. The total length of the building was 1,296 feet and the greatest width 492 feet. Jones's design is much more picturesque than any previous crystal palace designs on this scale . Some of the towers were undoubtedly intended to house tanks so as to provide a suitable head of water for fountains in the grounds, but it is difficult to conceive of a use for the others, which appear to have been included solely to enhance the effect of the silhouette. Their roofs, and that of the main dome, are distinctly Islamic in appearance, and reflect two further designs for the St Cloud site of which drawings also survive in the Victoria and Albert Museum.

Although the Muswell Hill project was officially inaugurated on 16 July 1859, it had fallen through by June of the following year. No doubt the experience of those involved with the Sydenham Crystal Palace, which had cost considerably more than expected, was a contributory factor. But, however much this may have disappointed Jones, it cannot have been for long because within a few months he was involved in the proposal to erect the building at St Cloud. The documentation of this project is sparse and difficult to follow. It seems likely that Jones and Joseph Paxton may have been members of a company, perhaps financed by Paxton's patron,

Baron Rothschild, formed to build the palace, and that at some time during 1862 this was dissolved and Jones dropped out. In spite of further attempts to form another company the project again fell through. In this instance perhaps it was the threat of competition from Lehmann and Peignet's Universal and Permanent Exhibition, which opened at Auteuil in 1863, which provided the reason.

Lit. J. Physick and M. Darby, *op. cit.,* p. 170.
M. Darby and D. van Zanten, *op. cit.,* pp. 60-65.

WYATT, Sir Matthew Digby (1820-1877)

70 Chimney piece.

Plate 224 in J.B. Waring, *Masterpieces of Industrial Art and Sculpture at the International Exhibition, 1862,* 1863.
Chromolithograph. 41.8 × 29.8.
Private Collection.

71 The Billiard Room at 12 Kensington Palace Gardens. 1864.

Photograph taken in c.1974. Courtesy of G.L.C..

After Sir Samuel Morton Peto completed his new house at 12A Kensington Palace Gardens, no. 12, the house which he had built for himself in 1845-6 to the designs of Charles Barry, was sold for £25,000 to Alexander Collie. Collie, a London and Manchester cotton merchant, employed Matthew Digby Wyatt in 1864 to make extensive alterations. The principal staircase was carried up to the second floor, a breakfast room was added at the north west corner, and this Moorish billiard room was built in what had previously been a kitchen. Collie continued to live in the house until 1875 when he broke bail and disappeared after his business had gone bankrupt and he had been prosecuted for obtaining £200,000 under false pretences.

Wyatt's inspiration is unclear. He did not have any direct contact apparently with Islamic architecture until visiting Spain after the room was completed, and apart from his design for the Museum of the East India Company which was based on the architecture of the Diwan-i-Khas, or Hall of Private Audience at Agra Fort, is not known to have carried out any other works in a similar style. Given the statement by the writer of his obituary in the *Builder* that 'between Owen Jones and Digby Wyatt who had many interests in common with him, there sprang up a friendship which seemed to have its public as well as its private phase; as it certainly happened whether accidentally or otherwise that the two men were working together continually throughout their life,' one cannot help but wonder whether Jones might have had a hand in the choice of style.

The immediate inspiration, however, may have been Collie's purchase of a fireplace at the International Exhibition of 1862 which he subsequently incorporated into the room. This was made by Maw and Company and designed by Wyatt, who was said by J.B. Waring, to have 'very tastefully adapted the style of the Alhambra'. Wyatt's involvement with Maw, who probably supplied the ceramic decoration for the remainder of the room, stemmed from the interest in tile design which he

70

had developed in the 1840s as a result of being employed by Jones's friend John Blashfield to make drawings of mosaic and tessellated floor designs in Italy. His work for Maw included the design of floors for the Law Courts, Toronto, Canada.

As depicted in this illustration the fireplace includes a grate which was never, in fact, associated with it. Waring explained that no grate was included in the exhibition and 'this deficiency we have ventured to make good in our drawing by inserting a portion of a cleverly designed grate exhibited by Mr Taylor.'

Lit. G.L.C. Survey of London, XXXVII, *Northern Kensington*, 1973, pp. 167-170, pl. 95d.

JONES, Owen (1809-1874)

72 Design for a wallpaper for John Trumble. March 1858.
Pen and ink and water-colour. 28.6 × 47.
Victoria and Albert Museum (D.77-1897).

73 Design for a wallpaper. c.1865.
Water-colour and gold paint. Sight size. 39.1 × 52.7.
Victoria and Albert Museum (8103).

Owen Jones's sister, Catherine, presented ten volumes of wallpapers designed by him to the Victoria and Albert Museum in 1877. These contain

some 1,345 examples, though many are different colour-ways of the same design, and include, besides papers dated 1852 by Townsend and Parker, examples by John Trumble and Sons, and Jeffery and Company. Many of Jones's original designs are also in the possession of the Museum.

John Trumble and Sons were founded in 1856 when Trumble and William Cooke split up their partnership and moved to different buildings in Leeds. Jones appears to have worked for them from 1858, the date on many of his designs, and in 1859 Trumble advertised that they were the 'sole manufacturers of Mr Owen Jones's new designs for 1859'. Jeffery and Company were founded in 1836 as Jeffery, Wise and Company, but Jones does not seem to have begun designing for them until after 1865, the year in which Jackson and Graham entrusted to Jeffery the printing of Jones's papers for the Viceroy's Palace at Cairo. From that date until his death Jones designed numerous papers for the firm, including an elaborate plaster design which helped to gain for them a Gold Medal at the Paris Exhibition of 1867. At the same time, Jeffery continued to make papers for Jackson and Graham, including no doubt, most of those for the schemes carried out to Jones's designs.

Jones had laid down his views on wallpaper in a lecture in 1852: 'It is very evident that one of the first principles to be attended to in adorning walls of an apartment, is that nothing should disturb their

71

flatness ... diaper patterns in self tints are safest ... but when varieties of colours are used, the Oriental rule of so interweaving the form and colour as that they may present a neutralised bloom when viewed at a distance, should never be departed from.'

Lit. A.V. Sugden and J.L. Edmondson, *History of English Wallpaper*, 1925.
O. Jones 'On the True and the False ...', 1852, pp. 78-80.

72

JONES, *Owen (1809-1874)*

74 'Culross', design for a woven textile.
Signed and dated *August 15 1870*. Numbered *5*.
Water-colour. 42.5 × 63.5.
Victoria and Albert Museum (T.562-1972).

75 'Culross', woven silk manufactured by Warner, Sillett and Ramm, Braintree.
54.7 × 52.8.
Victoria and Albert Museum (T.157-1972).

Like his wallpaper designs Jones's textile patterns are produced from a tight geometrical grid, exactly like those he had discerned in the Alhambra decorations. Sometimes these construction lines are allowed to remain, and become part of the pattern; sometimes parts are removed and the crossings become stars; sometimes they are elaborated and become stems and leaves; and sometimes they are removed altogether and the infill patterns, often borrowed from many different sources, form designs in their own right. In 1874 the *Furniture Gazette* remarked on the appropriateness of this type of design to machine production, and that is particularly obvious in some of Jones's silk designs where he cleverly allows the patterns inherent in the weaving process to form part of the design. Thus, the different shapes are distinguished by diagonal and horizontal stripes, zig zags and dots.

Jones's involvement with textiles began at least as early as 1851 when the *Journal of Design* included a sample of printed cotton which he had designed for Thomas De La Rue. His first woven textiles seem to have been those he designed for the Dunfermline firm of Erskine Beveridge called 'Alhambra', 'Arabesque' and 'Vine', which were shown in the Great Exhibition. Later, he contributed a chapter on textile design to J.B. Waring, *Art Treasures of the United Kingdom* (1858), and designed many woven silks for the Braintree firm of Benjamin Warner. When presenting this particular silk to the Victoria and Albert Museum, Sir Frank Warner wrote, that in preparing his first design for the firm, Jones had extended it onto the squared paper himself 'a task he found so arduous ... that he swore he would never do another.'

WARREN, *Albert Henry (1830-1911)*

76 Binding for *Lays of the Holy Land*, **1858.**
Cloth blocked in blue and gold by Leighton, Son and Hodge. 16.8 × 23.3.
Victoria and Albert Museum: National Art Library.

77 Binding for T. Moore, *Lalla Rookh*, **1860.**
Cloth blocked in blue and gold by Leighton, Son and Hodge. 17 × 23.
Victoria and Albert Museum: National Art Library.

Although the Moresque style is appropriate to the titles of these particular volumes, Warren's designs are typical of those he produced for many other bindings without oriental subjects. Of all Jones's pupils Warren learned to imitate his master's style most closely, and much of his work is consequently indistinguishable. Apart from cover designs he also did illustrations for *A Book of Favourite Modern Ballads* (1860), (also titled *Choice Pictures and Choice Poems* and *The Illustrated Poetical Gift Book*); *The Promises of Jesus Christ* (1860); *Ave Maria: A Figure of the Holy Virgin* (before November 1865); *Arms of the Episcopate of Great Britain*, with notes by the Reverend J. Woodward, (1868); and *A Book of Fruits and Blossoms for Little Folk to Paint* (1885). As a lithographer he assisted J.B. Waring with his *Masterpieces of Industrial Art and Sculpture at the International Exhibition 1862*, 186, and Owen Jones and his father with *Paradise and the Peri*, 1860 (nos. 79-80).

Lit. S. Pantazzi, 'Four Designers of English Publishers' Bindings', *Papers of the Bibliographical Society of America*, 1961, p. 93.

73

75

WARREN, Henry (1798-1879)

78 View of Jerusalem from Mount Moriah. c.1862.
Water-colour. 36.7 × 20.5.
Searight Collection.

Although he is said never to have visited the Near East, Warren's principal pictures throughout his life were of Eastern subjects. The first, 'An Encampment of Turkish Soldiers in the Desert of Nubia' was exhibited in 1840, and several hundred others quickly followed: 'The Dying Camel' in 1841; 'The Return of the Pilgrims from Mecca' in 1848,

described as 'a large composition of numerous figures picturesquely grouped showing so accurate a knowledge of Eastern manners, customs and dress as almost to make us incredulous about the fact that the artist had never visited the land of Mahommedan;' and so on. In order to achieve such accuracy Warren relied on studying camels and dromedaries at Regents Park Zoo; on hiring clothes from theatrical costumiers; and on friends such as Owen Jones and Joseph Bonomi to supply him with information and artefacts. This view of Jerusalem, for example, is engraved opposite p. 387 in Rev. J.F. Fleetwood, *Life of Our Lord ... Jesus Christ* (1862),

where it states that it is 'after Bonomi'. Presumably Bonomi did the original when he was in Jerusalem with Catherwood and Arundale in 1833 (nos. 19-23). With Bonomi too, Warren collaborated over the production of a 'grand Moving Panoramic Picture of the Nile' in the late 1840s, of which all that now survives is a handbook in the British Museum. Bonomi and Warren had studied sculpture together under Nollekens; in 1835 Warren had showed a portrait of Bonomi in Egyptian dress at the Royal Society of British Artists (no. 656), and, interestingly, the two men both married relatives of John Martin: Bonomi his daughter, and Warren his niece (see no. 11).

With Owen Jones too, Warren was long acquainted. He provided the illustrations for at least six of the books which Jones printed, starting with the plates in *Ancient Spanish Ballads* (no. 63) in 1841, and ending with the figures in *Scenes from a Winter's Tale* published in 1866. Warren also drew seven of the magnificent lithographs in Catherwood's *Views of Ancient Monuments in Central America, Chiapas and Yucatan* which Jones published in 1844. Warren's name appears too as an 'ornamental draughtsman' in Jones's Department at the Crystal Palace at Sydenham, and his son Albert Henry was one of Jones's most proficient pupils.

Lit. *Art Journal*, 1861, pp. 265-67; 1880, p.83.
Illustrated London News, 3 January 1880, p. 12.
A. Graves, *Royal Academy Exhibitors*, 1906.
R.Searight, *The Middle East*, 1971, no. 64, p. 21.

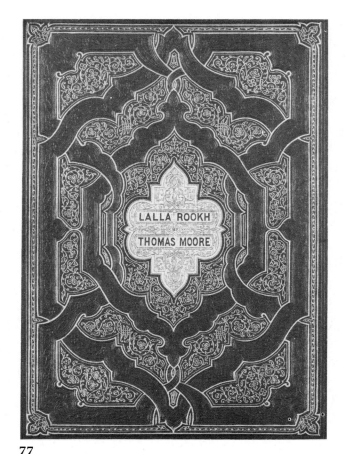

77

JONES, *Owen (1809-1874) and* WARREN, *Henry (1798-1879)*

79, 80 Two designs for pages in T. Moore, *Paradise and the Peri,* **1860.**
Water-colour. Size of page 24 × 32.7.
Private Collection.

Jones's interest in oriental ornament expanded in the early 1860s to embrace both Persian and Chinese designs. In the *Grammar of Ornament* (1856) he had pointed out that although Persian ornament combined the conventional with an attempt at the natural, it was much less pure than Arabian and Moresque ornament. It did, however, present 'considerable grandeur in the main features', and it is those features which Jones most used. He seems to have first re-considered Persian ornament when designing the decorative borders for this edition of Moore's *Paradise and the Peri* which was published by Day and Son in 1860, and includes figurative illustrations by Henry Warren. Several designs, those on the first and last pages, for example, and on pages 20 and 21 derive directly from Persian manuscripts such as that now in the Victoria and Albert Museum which Jones had used for plate XLVIII in the *Grammar.* Furthermore, an advertisement in the *Bookseller* 27 October 1860 confirmed that 'it is the intention of those concerned ... that it shall possess all the higher qualities of Oriental gorgeousness in colour and design.'

Paradise and the Peri was the first of three volumes in a similar format which Jones and Warren designed, and Day and Son printed and published. *The History of Joseph and his Brethren,* with Egyptian designs, appeared in 1862, and *Scenes from a Winter's Tale,* with eclectic designs including an Islamic element, in 1866.

78

79

80

These designs were probably lot 45 in the sale of Jones's drawings at Sotheby's on 19 June 1876, and may include one or more of those exhibited in the exhibition of Jones's works arranged at the London International Exhibition of 1874 (nos. 163, 164, 168).

JONES, Owen (1809-1874)

81 Menu for the banquet given by the foreign Commissioners for the Paris International Exhibition to the Imperial Commission on 26 October 1867.
Lettered *Thos. De La Rue & Co. London and Paris* and with details of courses, etc..
Chromolithograph. 29.3 × 45.3.
Private Collection.

Jones apparently designed the menu on the instructions of Henry Cole, for Cole recorded in his diary on 28 September 1867: 'O. Jones brought revised design in the evening.' That this is probably the menu he referred to is suggested by the presence of a folded copy among Cole's papers in the Victoria and Albert Museum, National Art Library. Both men were in Paris in 1867 for the International Exhibition, indeed, Jones had been awarded a gold medal for the furniture designs he had prepared for Jackson and Graham. The menu was printed by Thomas de la Rue – there is a copy in the De La Rue archive at Reading University – and the work was probably done in Paris, since the firm had a branch there.

Lit. M. Darby, *op. cit.*, 1974, pp. 453, 490.

JONES, Owen (1809-1874)

82 Calendar for the year 1869.
Water-colour and gouache with gold paint. Sight size 16 × 25.8.
Private Collection.

T.M. (An unknown pupil of Owen Jones.)

83 Calendar for the year 1879.
Signed on the back with a monogram of the letters TM. The dates are printed on separate sheets pasted on.
Water-colour and gouache with gold paint. 18 × 29.1.
Private Collection.

On the basis of their similarity to designs in the Library at Reading University, which Jones prepared for the firm of De La Rue, it is almost certain that he produced these calendar designs for that firm too. The writer of his obituary noted that 'he was long and largely connected' with De La Rue, and that 'he may be said to have metamorphosised everything in their establishment, and helped largely to give it the renown it has ever retained. He designed their playing cards, their stamps, – in fact, all that they produced.' This account does not exaggerate, from at least as early as 1844, until his death thirty years later, Jones played a prominent part in the lives of three generations of De La Rues. He not only designed their products, but their factories and houses also, and Warren William De La Rue, who took over the running of the firm with his two brothers after their father died in 1889, was apprenticed to Jones from 1864.

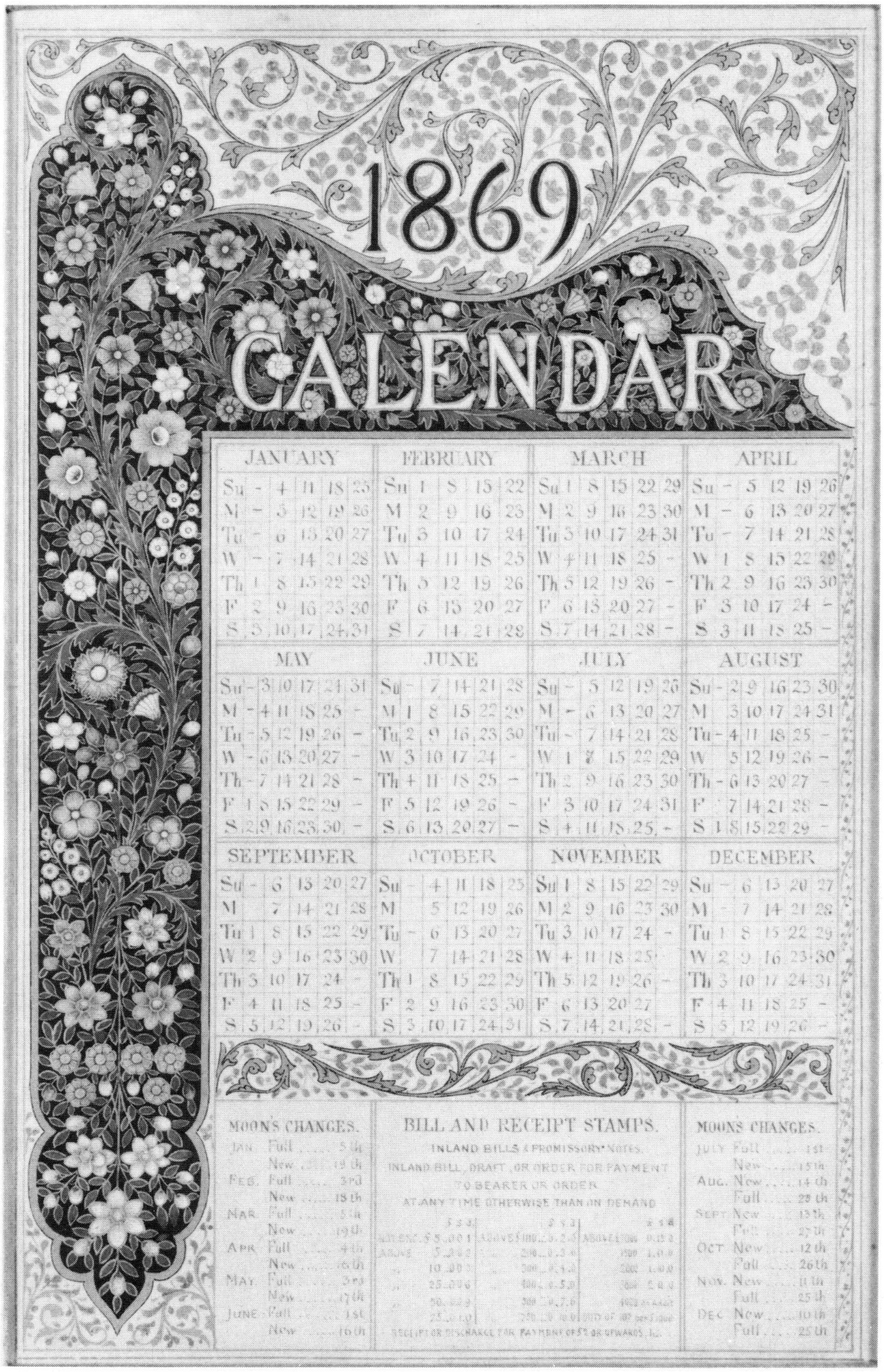

1869 CALENDAR

82

Jones's skill in adapting similar designs, many of them including an Islamic element, to many different types of product – playing cards, bank notes and stamps for many different countries, chess boards, diaries, at least four hundred bookbinding tools, watermarks, and monograms are some of those which he is known to have worked on – established a distinct 'house style' for De La Rue which appears to be among the first manifestations of a phenomenon which became widespread in the present century. It is on the basis of his concern for the aesthetic appearance of even the most trivial product, and on his packing designs like the biscuit tin labels he produced for Huntley and Palmer, that Jones is often said to have been the first commercial designer.

Lit. L. Houseman, *The House that Thomas Built*, 1968.
M. Darby, *op. cit.*, 1974, pp. 124-6.

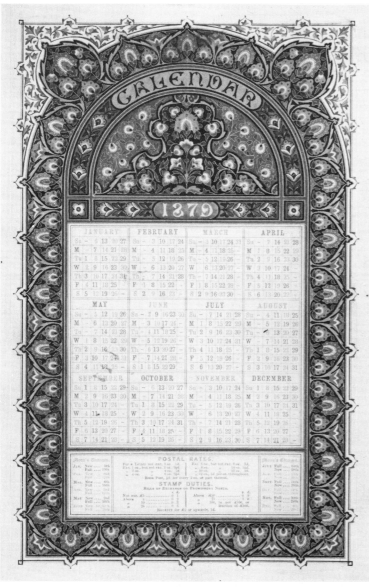

83

JONES, Owen (1809-1874)

84 Design for the decoration of a ceiling. c.1865.
Pencil, water-colour, and gold paint. 30.2 × 50.
Victoria and Albert Museum (E.1687-1912).

85 Ceiling; 16 Carlton House Terrace, London. 1866.
Modern photograph. Courtesy of Lonrho plc, owners of Crockford's Club.

86 Inlaid wooden door from a bookcase in the library at 16 Carlton House Terrace. c.1866.
Victoria and Albert Museum (W.43-1970).

In the last fifteen years of his life Owen Jones carried out many decorative schemes, often costing enormous sums of money, for various *nouveaux riches* middle class capitalists, some of whom were members of the companies which projected the crystal palaces he had hoped to build. Perhaps the most lavish of all were those he provided for Alfred

Morrison at 16 Carlton House Terrace between 1865 and 1870. Morrison, who was born in 1821, inherited a fortune amounting to several million pounds, and further increased this through the Fore Street firm of Morrison and Dillon, which was effectively the first departmental store in London to concentrate on making many small profits rather than few large ones. Jones had designed a dairy for Morrison's father in 1845, and in the early 1860s decorated, with the firm of Jackson and Graham, the interiors of Alfred's house at Fonthill (now demolished).

16 Carlton House Terrace was the last of the houses south of the Duke of York's steps added by Morton Peto, between 1863 and 1866, to Nash and Pennethorne's scheme of some thirty years earlier. Morrison acquired the lease on the 25 May 1865 and immediately called in Jackson and Graham, and Jones, and appears to have given them *carte blanche* to decorate the ground and first floors. Accounts of Morrison notice that he 'specially interested himself

84

85

art and were the inspiration for the work of Jackson and Graham, and Jones. They must certainly have lived up to Morrison's expectations, the decoration, much of which still survives, exhibits 19th century craftsmanship at the peak of its perfection. Monclure Conway wrote in his *Travels in South Kensington with notes on Decorative Art and Architecture in England* (1882) that 'the work need fear no comparison with any other, of whatever age or country. It makes the chief palaces of Northern Europe vulgar;' and Mrs Haweis, *Beautiful Houses* (1882), noticed that much of it was 'of the finest marquetries of inlaid natural woods and satisfactorily answers the common complaint that modern workmen cannot, or will not, do the good work which ancient workmen did ... The cost must have been tremendous.'

The decorations were apparently completed by May 1870 when Henry Cole visited Morrison, and wrote in his diary afterwards: 'To Mr Morrison's ... his house filled with marquetrie designed by Owen Jones ... mixture of Greek and Moorish, perfect mechanical work.' Cole's description sums up the mood of the decoration well. The general impression is one of a combination of Greek and Islamic forms, but it is not possible to point to specific sources for Jones's designs which contain many other elements besides; Chinese in the drawing room; Pompeian in the study; and an underlying naturalism in many details of the patterns. In spite of this naturalism Jones's designs are primarily geometrical. Straight lines are easier to manage than curved in inlaid work and painted decoration, and it is they which dominate the designs. This geometric bias, coupled with the chanceless perfection of Jackson and Graham's

to seek out artistic craftsmen in all countries, and employed them for years in the slow and careful production of master-pieces of cameo cutting, inlaying of metals, and enamelled glass.' One of these craftsmen was the Islamic metalworker Zuloaga. Minute detail and craftsmanship of the highest quality characterised his taste for decorative

86

Jones's work reflected his client's earnest academicism, and the rooms, when hung with the Morrison's large collection of embroideries, lace and other textiles, must have appeared very sumptuous. Jones and Morrison had, in fact, arrived at a kind of 'aesthetic' interior embodying the 'orientalism' of the better-known designs of Godwin, Whistler and others, but they had taken a very different route.

16 Carlton House Terrace is presently leased to The Terrace Club.

Lit. M. Darby, *op. cit.*, 1974, pp. 415-25, and sources cited therein.

WYATT, Sir Matthew Digby (1820-1877)

87 Drawings (6) of the Casa Alba and Casa de los Abbades, Seville, the Alcazar, Segovia, and the Casa de Las Conchas, Salamanca, made while on a tour of Spain in 1869, and subsequently published as illustrations in the artist's An Architect's Note-Book in Spain Principally Illustrating the Domestic Architecture of that Country, **1872.**
Each inscribed with title, and initialled and dated *MDW 1869*.
Pen and ink. Each 13 × 15.5.
Victoria and Albert Museum (9048.1-6).

Wyatt begins his book with a touching dedication to Owen Jones: 'My Dear Owen, The last book I wrote I dedicated to my brother by blood; the present I dedicate to you – my brother in Art. Let it be a record of the value I set upon all you have taught me, and upon your true friendship.' As evidence of what he had learned Wyatt, in the introductory text to his views of the Alhambra, quoted extensively from the *Grammar of Ornament* (1856) and concluded: 'these words are ... those ... of the man who better, I believe, than any other living man understands the subject upon which he is speaking. His knowledge too is not that of the theorist only; as a practical designer he has tested the applicability of the lessons he has derived from his studies; and shown that such studies lead to certain and foreknown results of great beauty, applicable to the Arts and Industries of the Present, as he traced their perfect harmony in days of old with the Arts and Industries of the Past.'

When Wyatt's book was published both men were in the last years of their lives, Jones died two years later, in 1874, and Wyatt three years after that. Although Wyatt had apparently not visited Spain before there is a strong element of nostalgia in his writing, as if he had lived with the Alhambra all his life but had, nevertheless, to return to it before death: 'As the moonlight caught the snow-clad peaks of the Sierra Nevada and traced itself in the silver lines of the winding River Genil, coming from the far off distance to the city beneath, and losing itself in the thousands of twinkling lights of the suburbs in which its silver threads seemed to get entangled and lost, everything was perfect; and as one turned away towards the nearer mountain heights, and saw upon their hilly eastern slopes, the Generalife and the Alhambra, almost close at hand, one felt inclined to forget the present in the past and to think of ruin as perfecton, and of death as life.'

craftsmanship does give an undeniably mechanical and lifeless quality to much of the work, which is further emphasised by the lack of large areas of colour. The range of colours provided by even the most catholic assortment of rare woods is still limited by comparison with a selection of paints, and although small areas of red, green and gold appear in the ceilings, the general impression is subdued when compared with the sparkling interiors of the St James's Hall or Osler's Gallery (no. 68).

87

SECTION 3

OWEN JONES AND HIS CIRCLE

Part 2
Principles and Practical Art

In the text to plate 37 of *Plans, Details, Elevations and Sections of the Alhambra* (1842-6) Owen Jones makes an extraordinary statement about the system of polychromy used by the early architects: 'the colours employed were, in all cases, the primitive blue, red and yellow (gold); the secondary colours, purple, green and orange, arising only in the mosaic dadoes, which being nearer the eye, formed a point of repose from the brilliant colouring above ... it may be remarked that among the Arabs, the Egyptians, and the Greeks, the primitive colours, if not exclusively employed, were certainly nearly so, during the early periods of art; whilst during the decadence, the secondary colours became of more importance.' Interestingly this observation had a direct parallel in the work which scientists were doing on colour. Sir David Brewster, who re-discovered the kaleidoscope in 1815,[1] utilised the earlier work of Newton to prove that red, yellow and blue were the primary colours; and George Field, the chemist, showed in his *Chromotography; or a Treatise on Colours and Pigments and their Powers in Painting* (1835) that correct combinations of these colours could produce white light.

The co-incidence of these separate conclusions apparently remained unnoticed by Jones, until 1850 when he was asked to decorate the Crystal Palace. The story of the commission is told in the catalogue (no. 88); how Jones used red, yellow and blue to elevate the building to the same standing as the Alhambra and the Parthenon; how he evolved a formula for applying the colours to the ironwork of Barry and Paxton based on the work of the scientists on light; and how the result related directly to the Eastern experiences which had first motivated him. Thus, Jones came to realise that it was not the forms of Islamic decorations themselves which held the key to the development of a 'new style', but the principles which lay behind them.

Others before Jones had written of principles. Charles Heath Wilson, a director of the Schools of Design in 1843, spoke of the importance of assembling 'examples of ornamental manufactures ... in order to exhibit ... the actual practical application of the principles of design in the arrangement of forms and harmony in the combination of colours.'[2] Pugin published his *True Principles of Pointed or Christian Architecture* in 1841; James Fergusson, *The Principles of Beauty of Art with reference to Architecture* in 1849, and Edward Garbett his *Rudimentary Treatise on the Principles of Design in Architecture* in 1850. These writers believed that there were certain principles governing design and ornament which transcended time and national frontiers, but they made little attempt to be more specific. This was where Jones differed. He had had the enervating experience of success in applying particular examples, and immediately realised the possibility of drawing up a set of 'rules', which would not only act as guidelines for modern development, but would also ensure that Victorian design related directly to that of the Egyptians, the Greeks and the Moors.

Jones's utilitarian approach to design was reflected in the establishment of the Department of Practical Art in 1852, (the name changed to Science and Art in the following year), a separate section of the Board of Trade with responsibility for administering the Schools of Design and a Museum of Ornamental Art. The Superintendent and main mover behind the setting up of the new Department was Henry Cole, Jones's employer at the Crystal Palace, and it is hardly surprising, therefore, to read in Cole's diary, now in the Victoria and Albert Museum, that on the 29 March 1852 he was discussing a 'professorship' with Jones. In the event, Jones did not accept this post, but he did work closely with Cole in developing his concept of 'principles'. That British goods had made such a poor showing at the Great Exhibition confirmed the need for the radical changes in the teaching philosophy of the Schools which Cole had already advocated, and 'principles' could play an important role in the new programme. By 28 April 1852 Jones was able to lecture to the Society of Arts on 'An Attempt to Define the Principles which should Regulate the Employment of Colour in the Decorative Arts', in which he listed nineteen specific axioms;[3] and in June 1852, he gave a series of four lectures at Marlborough House, the home of the Department, entitled 'On the True and False in the Decorative Arts', in which he added a further four, elaborating fitness and form.[4] The Marlborough House lectures were subsequently published by the Department as their official doctrine, and Jones's principles were emblazoned on the walls of the new museum.

The inspiration for the formulation of the 'principles', which were the guiding force for a whole generation of design students in the 1850s, was derived by Jones from his studies of Islamic ornament. The concept emerged from his work on the Alhambra as applied to the decoration of the Crystal Palace, and the first tentative formulation of specific axioms appeared in an article entitled 'Gleanings from the Great Exhibition of 1851. On the distribution of form and colour developed in the articles exhibited in the Indian, Egyptian, Turkish and Tunisian Departments', which was published in Cole's *Journal of Design and Manufactures* in 1851. This listed six principles:

'1 The construction is decorated; decoration is never purposely constructed.

2 Beauty of form is produced by lines growing out one from another in gradual undulations; there are no excrescences; nothing could be removed and leave the design equally good or better.

3 The general form is first cared for; this is subdivided and ornamented by general lines; the interstices are then filled with ornament, which is again subdivided and enriched for closer inspection.

4 Colour is used to assist in the development of form, and to distinguish objects, or parts of objects, one from another.

5 And to assist light and shade, helping the undulations of form by the proper distribution of the several colours; no artificial shadows are ever used.

6 That these objects were best obtained by the use of the primaries on small surfaces, or in small amounts, supported and balanced by the secondary and tertiary colours on the larger masses.'

The later principles elaborated on these, introducing the research of Field and Chevreul, as well as the work of Jones's fellow architects Pugin and Matthew Digby Wyatt.

The complete set of Principles as published in the *Grammar of Ornament*, itself an aid to 'practical art', and heavily biased in favour of Islamic design (nos. 99-104), lay their main stress on 'fitness', 'harmony' and 'proportion', and the 'repose' which these could engender. On fitness Jones proclaimed the primacy of the architectural form, from which all the decorative arts 'arise', and upon which they should be 'properly attendant'; and on proportion, he confirmed the importance of the work of Field; but it was to harmony that he devoted most attention. With regard to harmony of colour, he noticed the importance of the primaries, and concluded: 'the various objects should be blended so that the objects coloured, when viewed at a distance, should present a neutralised bloom.' This was what he observed in the Alhambra and what he succeeded in producing in his decoration of the Crystal Palace. To achieve harmony of form, ornament should be based upon a geometrical construction consisting of correctly balanced and contrasted straight, curved and inclined lines'; whereas beauty of form was produced by lines 'growing out from one another in gradual undulations'.

Jones's concept of repose, that enigmatic quality which the application of the principles was intended to produce, was apparently also based on his Eastern perceptions. In surveying many of the Islamic items in the Great Exhibition which were subsequently purchased by the Museum (nos. 89-94) he noted that there was 'no superfluous ornament', 'no struggle after effect', the ornament arises 'quietly and naturally from the want which has to be supplied' and the result was a 'sensation of most voluptuous repose'.[5] The wording and phraseology is similar to that in his 1835 lecture where he refers to the 'fairy halls of the golden palace of the Alhambra', which typified: 'the calm voluptuous translations of the Koran's doctrines'. Repose was not simply a visual quality but a spiritual one too. It was the 'true beauty' which 'the mind feels when the eye, the intellect, and the affections, are satisfied from the absence of any want.' Thus, the plates of *Ancient Spanish Ballads* (no. 63) should be seen both with the real eye and with the 'mind's eye', and the visitor to the Crystal Palace should experience the effect of the building by allowing his gaze to travel from the 'extreme brightness' in the foreground to the 'hazy indistinctness which Turner alone can paint'. It is perhaps in these terms too that Jones's frequently quoted remark that 'form without colour is like a body without soul' becomes comprehensible.[6]

Jones and the Departments of Practical Art, and Science and Art attempted to animate ornament, and to establish that 'principles' were as important to the manufacturer as the raw materials themselves. Their success is difficult to judge, simply because it cannot be measured in terms of its dependence upon Islamic prototypes. By the early 1860s, the Department's advocacy of oriental patterns founded on strict geometrical grids was already beginning to give way to the figurative ornament of the High Renaissance. In the work of Christopher Dresser (nos. 104-106), who constantly acknowledged his debt to Jones, one can perhaps detect the ultimate expression of the Department's doctrine. His flat pattern designs develop the over-heated ornament of Jones's mature 'new style' into powerful and compelling images; while it has frequently been said of his three dimensional designs that they are assertively 20th century in appearance.

Matthew Digby Wyatt writing about 'Orientalism in European Industry' in 1870 certainly believed that he could detect the influence of the East and that it was growing rather than receding: 'we work now in almost all departments of production, especially in carpets, rugs, tiles, floor-cloth, mural decoration, paper hangings, shawls and to some extent in jewellery and mosaics, in the spirit if not in the forms of Oriental art. Its influence is a growing and, as I believe, a highly beneficial one.'[7] But, while Wyatt, like Jones, advocated the acceptance of machine production and of science in general, John Ruskin, William Morris and others preached against the industrial system in favour of hand production.

102

Morris owned a copy of Jones's *Grammar of Ornament*, and his own patterns do adhere to many of Jones's principles of form and distribution, if not to those of colour. Secondaries and tertiaries impinging directly upon each other predominate in his textile and wallpaper designs, with the result that they appear much less formal, and more natural, than the designs of Jones – one might almost say more English than Eastern.

Notes

1 D.Brewster, *The Kaleidoscope: its History, Theory and Construction*, 1819. He records that 300,000 were sold in three months in London and Paris, and that large cargoes were sent elsewhere.
2 *Minutes of the Government School of Design*, 1849, pp. 284-85.
3 Reprinted in O. Jones, *Lectures on Architecture and the Decorative Arts*, 1863.
4 The lectures are listed in *First Report of the Department of Practical Art*, 1853, p. 228.
5 *Journal of Design and Manufactures*, June 1851, p. 91.
6 This remark was apparently first made in a speech at a banquet to mark the opening of the Fishmongers Hall in June 1866 after it had been re-decorated by Jones.
7 *Macmillan's Magazine*, 126, April 1870, pp. 551-556.

88

SIMPSON, William (1823-1829)

88 Owen Jones's scheme for the decoration of the Great Exhibition building, 1850.

Pen and ink and water-colour. Sight size 71 × 99.
Victoria and Albert Museum (546-1897).

By the time construction of Paxton's Crystal Palace had started in 1850, Owen Jones had been appointed one of the 'Superintendents of Works', and was being assisted by his pupils Jacob Wrey Mould and Albert Henry Warren, and his brother-in-law James William Wild. At the same time Matthew Digby Wyatt was responsible for general tasks concerning the exhibits, and Charles Heard Wild, James William's brother, for checking calculations and testing the structural members of the building. Jones's work was to involve the decoration and interior arrangement, but in practice he did rather more than that, designing the iron railing around the building in a Moorish fretwork, and other details.

The interior decoration of the Crystal Palace has been little studied, and is interesting in the context of this exhibition, for in devising what colours to use and how to apply them Jones adopted the principles used by the Moors in decorating the Alhambra. Initially, he wrote to some twenty architects soliciting their views as to the best way to paint Paxton's iron work. When no two agreed he proceeded to invent a system of his own, painting

three groups of columns in the partially completed structure in different manners; one with a neutral tint, one plain red, and one in stripes of red, yellow and blue separated by narrow lines of white. At the same time he also painted a portion of the roof red, yellow and blue, again separating the colours with white, and confining the red to the underside of the girders. These trial schemes were inspected by Prince Albert and the Royal Commissioners on 5 December 1850 with this and another painting which had been ordered by Jones to show the overall effect. Jones later explained that the red and neutral columns had never been part of his scheme but had been prepared in obedience to the wishes of some critics who thought the red, yellow and blue columns would be unsatisfactory.

The Commissioners accepted the red, yellow and blue scheme with some minor alterations, and this immediately provoked an uproar in the press from critics who were certain that the effect would be disastrous. The *Art Journal* summarised the general view: 'small strips of colour in violent contrast in all directions will be both painful and unsightly ... we must protest in the strongest terms, against the commonplace vulgarity of the conception, added to its other evils will be the injury it will do the colours of a majority of the goods exhibited'. What the *Builder* eventually dubbed 'The Great Paint Question' was posed, and a flood of letters to various journals sought to put Jones right, suggestions ranging from Frederick Sang's that the glass be coloured and the metalwork painted a bronze green, to that of 'An Artist' that the ironwork be painted in superimposed glazes to achieve a vibrant grey similar to that in Titian's paintings. Criticism continued to mount at such an alarming rate, the *Times* commenting that an unfavourable impression was produced on 'nearly all' who saw the trial bays, that Jones was obliged to defend his views in a lecture before a packed audience at the Royal Institute of British Architects on 16 December 1850.

The immediate problem of deciding what colours to use, he explained, could be solved by reference to archaeological sources. Then it was found that the primaries always predominated during early periods, but, as these civilisations declined, so secondary and tertiary colours began to prevail. On the relevant proportions of the colours Jones stated that: 'Mr Field in his admirable works on colour, has shown by direct experiment, that white light consists of blue, red and yellow, neutralising each other in the proportions of 8, 5, 3. It will be readily seen that the nearer we can arrive at this state of neutrality the more harmonious and light giving will a building become; and an examination of the most perfect specimens of harmonious colouring of the ancients will show that this proportion has generally obtained.' As to how these primaries should be applied: 'blue, which relieves' was to be placed 'on the concave surfaces; yellow, which advances, on the convex; and red, the colour of the middle distance, on the horizontal planes.' Furthermore, Jones proposed 'in all cases to interpose a line of white between them'. This last was also observed in the works of antiquity and was confirmed as ideal by the recent research of the French scientist Michel Chevreul on the 'simultaneous contrast' of colours.

In adopting red, yellow and blue Jones could justifiably claim that he was using the colours adopted by the Greeks, Egyptians, and the Moors, but once he went further than that to 'the most perfect specimens of harmonious colouring of the ancients', and to discuss proportions of colour and methods of application, he had to rely almost entirely on his work on the Alhambra, for only in that building did sufficient evidence of colour survive to enable such calculations to be made.

Jones's lecture failed to convince many of his critics and the battle continued to rage, George Godwin, the editor of the *Builder*; the decorators Leonard Collman and John Crace, Edward Rippingille, the painter, and others, joining in. In the meantime, Jones went quietly ahead with his scheme, or as the *Times* put it, he continued 'perversely'. By 15 January, however, when all structural work and a part of the painting of the transept roof had been completed, the first hint of a change of attitude in the press became evident. One week later Henry Cole reported that Prince Albert had visited the site and 'liked the colouring', and by the time it was completed praise was being heaped upon Jones from all quarters. The *Times* reluctantly admitted that 'Mr Jones will, after all, maintain, if not increase his reputation as a decorator' and the *Illustrated London News* stated that 'on entering the

south transept a spectacle is afforded which fills the mind with wonder and produces an overwhelming effect upon the senses ... as the eye wanders up the vistas the three primitive colours ... red, yellow, and blue, strike the eye by the intensity of their brightness in the foreground; but by blending in the distance, by the effect of parallax and diminished angle, the whole as in nature disappears into a neutral grey. To appreciate the genius of Owen Jones, the visitor must take his stance at the extremity of the building ... looking up the nave, with its endless rows of pillars, the scheme vanishes from extreme brightness to the hazy indistinctness which Turner alone can paint.'

Thus, by utilising his archaeological work on Islamic decoration and relating it to the scientific work of Chevreul and Field, Jones succeeded in realising the general intention of his earlier work, to create a vibrant, atmospheric architecture evoking the grandeur and luminosity of an oriental experience. Had the hangings shown in this picture been carried out, then perhaps they might have combined with the carpets to give the impression of a bazaar, and thus to have further emphasised the eastern atmosphere. They were apparently conceived by Jones as an ingenious method of providing a barrel vaulted effect to the nave at little expense, and are, surprisingly, not mentioned in either contemporary or later literature about the exhibition.

Lit. J. Physick and M. Darby, *op. cit.*, pp. 166-8.
   M. Darby and D. van Zanten, *op. cit.*, pp. 53-75, and sources cited therein.

DELAMOTTE, Philip Henry

89 Indian scarf end embroidered at Dacca on white muslin. Shown at the Great Exhibition, 1851.
Plate 48 in M. Digby Wyatt, *The Industrial Arts of the Nineteenth Century*, 1853.
Inscribed with title and P.H. Dellamotte, [sic] del. F. Bedford. ·d. Lith. M. Digby Wyatt, Dirext. London. Printed and Published March 15th 1852 by Day & Son, Lithographers to the Queen.
Chromolithograph. Size of page 33.5 × 48.5.
Private Collection.

ANONYMOUS

90 Group of Indian objects, principally enamelled. Shown at the Great Exhibition, 1851.
Plate 152 in M. Digby Wyatt, *The Industrial Arts of the Nineteenth Century*, 1853.
Inscribed with title and F. Bedford. Lith. M. Digby Wyatt, Dirext. London. Printed and Published March 1st 1853 by Day & Son Lithographers to the Queen.
Chromolithograph. Size of page 33.5 × 48.5.
Private Collection.

91 Vessel and cover made in Lahore. c.1850.
Silver, enamelled. H. 24.2 D. 9.6.
Victoria and Albert Museum (128-1852).
Note: this is one of the objects illustrated in no. 90.

92 Rosewater sprinkler; Lucknow style but acquired as Rajasthani work from Dholpur. c.1850.
Silver, enamelled. H. 24.2 × 9.6.
Victoria and Albert Museum (130-1852).
Note: this is one of the objects illustrated in no.

89

93 Base of a *huqqa* **(water pipe) made in Purnea. c.1850.**
Bidri (blackened alloy inlaid with silver). H. 21.9 D. 23.5.
Victoria and Albert Museum (135-1852).

94 Base of a *huqqa* **(water pipe) made in Hyderabad. c.1850.**
Bidri (blackened alloy inlaid with silver). H. 22.6 D. 12.4.
Victoria and Albert Museum (139-1852).
Note: Nos. 91-94 were purchased by the Museum at the Great Exhibition in 1851.

When the Government offered £5,000 to Henry Cole for the purchase of items from the Great Exhibition to form the nucleus of a Museum of Ornamental Art – what is now the Victoria and Albert Museum – he

93

91

quickly set up a selection committee consisting of Richard Redgrave, A.W.N. Pugin, Owen Jones and himself. They met four times in the winter of 1851/2, Pugin, then close to death, travelling up from Ramsgate to be at the Exhibition by 7 o'clock in the morning. Although not all the money was spent several hundred objects were selected, and a catalogue with prices was written by Jones and published as an Appendix to the *First Report of the Department of Practical Art*, 1853.

This collection has not been the subject of serious study. When one adds up the numbers of objects in each category, and the prices paid, interesting figures emerge which reveal that there was a strong bias towards Islamic items. For example, £1,276 was spent on objects from India as opposed to only £865. 11s. 5d. on those from England. Of the £996. 14s. 4d. spent on textiles, the *Art Journal* noticed in July 1852 that they were 'with one or two exceptions, entirely of Eastern manufacture'; and of the £1,371 6s. 0d. on metalwork, the major portion was also devoted to Near Eastern and Indian artefacts. Critics naturally baulked at this choice, there had been 1,788 exhibitors of textiles in the British Department alone, why were not some of these represented, or silks from Lyons or ribbons from St Etienne, instead, for example, of the horse accoutrements from Lahore which had cost £100?

The rationale behind the Committee's choice was explained by Jones some years later in the *Grammar of Ornament* (1856): 'The Exhibition of the Works of Industry of all Nations in 1851 was barely opened to the public ere attention was directed to the gorgeous contributions of India. Amid the general disorder apparent in the application of Art to manufactures,

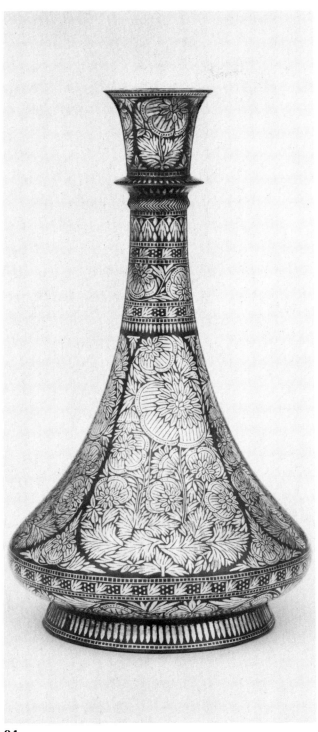

94

found but a fruitless struggle after novelty, irrespective of fitness ... there were to be found in isolated collections at the four corners of the transept all the principles, all the unity, all the truth, for which we had looked elsewhere in vain, and this because we were amongst a people practising an art which had grown up with their civilisation and strengthened with their growth. United by a common faith, their art had necessarily a common expression varying in each according to the influence to which each nation was subject. The Tunisian still retaining the art of the Moors who created the Alhambra; the Turk exhibiting the same art, but modified by the character of the mixed population over which they rule; the Indian uniting the severest forms of the Arabian art with the graces of Persian refinement.'

Jones and the other members of the Committee were not alone in considering the Islamic items superior, Matthew Digby Wyatt devoted a whole section to Indian objects in his *Industrial Arts of the Nineteenth Century* (1853) and Dr Waagen, the Director of the Museum at Berlin, also praised them above all others in his *Report on the Great Exhibition* (1852).

What Islamic ornament offered was a strong, naturally disciplined approach, producing 'appropriate' flat pattern design lacking in the products of most Western manufacturers. It is not difficult to understand public criticism of the Committee's choice, however. Many considered Indian art to be of 'ethnological' interest, and as such not suitable for inclusion in a museum of 'civilised' objects. Furthermore, a museum of Indian objects administered by the East India Company, already existed in London – and was provided with a new installation by Matthew Digby Wyatt from 1855. Although Jones further emphasised his point by opening the *Grammar of Ornament* (1856) with a chapter devoted to the ornament of savage tribes, and thereby rubbed salt in the wound, the Department was already showing signs of giving way on its insistence on 'principles' and non-figurative decoration. By the time that the new Museum buildings opened in the 1860s the emphasis was emphatically on the High Renaissance, and few Islamic objects were displayed.

FOLEY, John Henry (1818-1874)

95 Asia; marble group at one corner of the Albert Memorial, London. 1864-72.
Plate opposite page 24 in W. Cosmo Monkhouse, *The Works of John Henry Foley R.A.* (1875).
Engraving. 26.6 × 33.9.
Private Collection.

The intention of the eight large groups of statuary at the corners of the Albert Memorial was to reflect the Prince Consort's involvement in the success of the Great Exhibition of 1851. Thus, Asia commemmorated the contribution of China, Persia, India and Turkey, which are depicted as figures surrounding Asia herself seated on an elephant. The concept of five figures and an animal was suggested

the presence of so much unity of design, so much skill and judgement in its application, with so much of elegance and refinement in the execution as was observable in all the works not only of India, but all the other Mohammedan contributing countries, – Tunis, Egypt, and Turkey, – excited a degree of attention from artists, manufacturers, and the public, which has not been without its fruits. Whilst the works contributed by the various nations of Europe there were everywhere to be observed an entire absence of any common principle in the application of Art to Manufactures – whilst from one end to the other of the vast structure there could be

95

by G.G. Scott, the architect, while the general arrangement and massing were worked out by the sculptor H.H. Armstead, whom Scott employed to make small models some time before April 1864. Foley finished his own model based on Armstead's

sketch by November of the same year when it was approved by the Queen, and the final work was completed and installed after various delays by 1872.

Foley, echoing the early philosophy of the

Department of Practical Art, stated that his aim in his group of Asia was a 'general feeling of repose'. Most commentators accepted that he had achieved this, and declared his group the best of the four depicting the quarters of the globe, although the *Times* thought that some of the details were 'full of incongruity and barbarity'. The figure of Asia unveiling herself was misunderstood by at least one reviewer who suggested that she was removing her clothes for a 'dip in the Ganges'. Although shown draped in Armstead's original model, and in Foley's early sketch model, he eventually decided to depict her unveiling herself in 'allusion to the important display of the products of Asia, which was made at the Great Exhibition of 1851.'

Interestingly, Foley turned to both Joseph Bonomi and Henry Warren, as well as to A.H. Layard, for help over the details. On 24 July 1866 he wrote to Layard, for example, to thank him for the Persian ink and pen stand, and cup which will be 'of much service'; and on 15 December, in the same year, he wrote again explaining that he had seen Bonomi 're Dromedary saddle – unfortunately this is no more than the woodwork and therefore of little use ... I begin to feel I must be content to work from drawings which I shall no doubt be able to get from John Lewis or Henry Warren.' Layard himself was thanked on 7 March 1868 for lending an inscription to assist Foley in carving the Qur'an.

Lit. Layard correspondence in the British Museum.
   Saturday Review, 13 July 1872, p. 51.
   G.L.C. Survey of London, XXXVIII, *The Museums Area of South Kensington and Westminster*, 1975.

DELAMOTTE, Philip Henry (d. 1889)

96 The Alhambra Court at the Crystal Palace at Sydenham. 1854.
Photograph. 28 × 23.1.
Victoria and Albert Museum (39-316).

After the closure of the Great Exhibition in Hyde Park in 1851 Owen Jones and Matthew Digby Wyatt were employed under Joseph Paxton to act as Directors of Decoration for the re-erection of the building in a revised form at Sydenham, and thereby seduced temporarily away from the rival South Kensington Museum with which both had previously been involved. The complex story of their work, and of the building of the Fine Arts Courts largely to their designs, still remains to be told. Suffice it to say that Jones suggested that one of the courts should represent Islamic architecture, and as one would have surmised, he chose the

96

Alhambra as his model.

Originally it was intended to open the building on 1 May 1853, but as a result of delays this date was postponed by a year. On 18 November 1853 Queen Victoria visited the works and 'Mr Owen Jones pointed out ... the coloured restoration of one of the friezes of the Parthenon ... The Alhambra was not sufficiently advanced for inspection, but some of the pieces that are to form the honeycombed roof of the inner hall, which will require 5,000, were shown to Her Majesty.' By February 1854 the Alhambra Court was still behind schedule but, nevertheless, an opening date was fixed for 24 May. With only a few days to go, however, it was feared that although the Alhambra Court 'is beginning to put forth its beauties ... we are afraid it cannot be completed within the time'. The German Gothic Court, too, was behind, and it was decided to postpone the opening again, this time until 10 June. Even then the Alhambra Court was still not ready, and on the Monday after the opening ceremony 'twenty to thirty gilders were still at work'. These views may have been taken by Delamotte whose *Photographic Views of the Progress of the Crystal Palace, Sydenham*, was published in 1853.

Lit. M. Darby, *op. cit.*, 1974, pp. 331-346.

JONES, Owen (1809-1874)

97 Design for a detail of the decoration of the oriental courts, South Kensington Museum. 1863.
Water-colour, Chinese white and gold paint. Sight size 32.7 × 53.7.
Victoria and Albert Museum (E.3612-1931).

98 Design for the decoration of one bay of the oriental courts, South Kensington Museum. 1863.
Stamped *Science and Art Dept. 7 May 1863* and numbered *6803*.
Pen and ink, and water-colour. Sight size 45 × 46.4.
Victoria and Albert Museum (E.3608-1931).

A feature of the early buildings of the South Kensington Museum was their highly decorated interiors which included the present Morris, Gamble and Poynter Rooms, and the ceramic staircase and gallery. Like the ceramic gallery, which has now been stripped of its polychrome ornament, the oriental courts designed by Owen Jones, (now hidden from public gaze as the kitchens of the present restaurant), have also been deprived of their polychrome ornament.

Henry Cole first consulted Jones about the decoration of the oriental courts in May 1863. Four and a half months later Jones's designs for the Indian court were completed and he received £179. 7s. 0d. in payment for them. At the same time the tender of Thomas Kershaw, a decorator Jones had used elsewhere, for £350 for carrying out the work was accepted. By October the Museum was 'closed for works', and Jones was busy on his designs for the adjacent Chinese and Japanese courts. These were ready by the 26 February in the following year when another tender from Kershaw for their decoration

was accepted. By 14 May when Jones received £26. 5s. 0d. for 'superintending the decorations of the Indian Court' that was probably complete, but the Chinese and Japanese courts were not ready until after 6 April 1865 when Cole noted in his diary that Jones's work was 'nearly finished'. One reason for this apparent delay may have been Jones's complaints about 'bad workmanship'. For some reason which is not clear the court with the Moorish decorations does not seem to have been carried out, perhaps it was the lack of objects to go into it, or Jones's despair over the quality of Kershaw's work.

Unfortunately no contemporary illustrations of the oriental courts as completed are known. Apart from Jones's work they also included a 'Cairene' window designed by James Wild, which has now been removed but which can probably be identified with a drawing amongst those given to the Museum in 1928 by his daughter, and a mosaic portrait of Jones erected after his death.

The oriental courts were well received by critics. The *Building News*, for example, noted that although they were not so elaborate or so splendid as some of Jones's other works they were nevertheless successful. 'It was no easy task to devise a species of "wall veil" which would accommodate itself to the ugly outline of a modern segmental-headed window, and we think Mr Jones has done judiciously in tinting his piers with flat colour and reserving the richer portion of his design for the spandrels.'

Other drawings for the Chinese and Japanese courts in the Museum were bought by Christopher Dresser at the sale of Jones's drawings in 1875, and were subsequently acquired for the Museum from his executors.

Lit. *Précis of the Board Minutes of the Science and Art Department.*
12th *Report of the Science and Art*, 1865.
Building News, 5 May 1865.

WARREN, Albert Henry, AUBERT, Charles and STUBBS

Original drawings for O. Jones, *Grammar of Ornament*, 1856.

99 Arabian no. 3. Plate XXXIII.
Drawings (16) cut out and pasted onto a single sheet.
Pencil, pen and ink, wash, and Chinese white. Largest 19.7 × 20.
Victoria and Albert Museum (1606).

100 Turkish no. 1. Plate XXXVI.
Pen and ink and water-colour. Sight size 30.6 × 457.7.
Victoria and Albert Museum (1609).

101 Moresque no. 3. Plate XLI.
Drawings (12) cut out and pasted onto a single sheet.
Water-colour and gold paint. Largest 6.8 × 10.8.
Victoria and Albert Museum (1614).

102 Persian no. 3. Plate XLVI.
Drawings (25) cut out and pasted onto a single sheet.
Pen and ink, water-colour and gold paint. Largest 21.1 × 6.8.
Victoria and Albert Museum (1619).

97

98

99

PLATE XXXVI.

TURKISH. (N° 1)

100

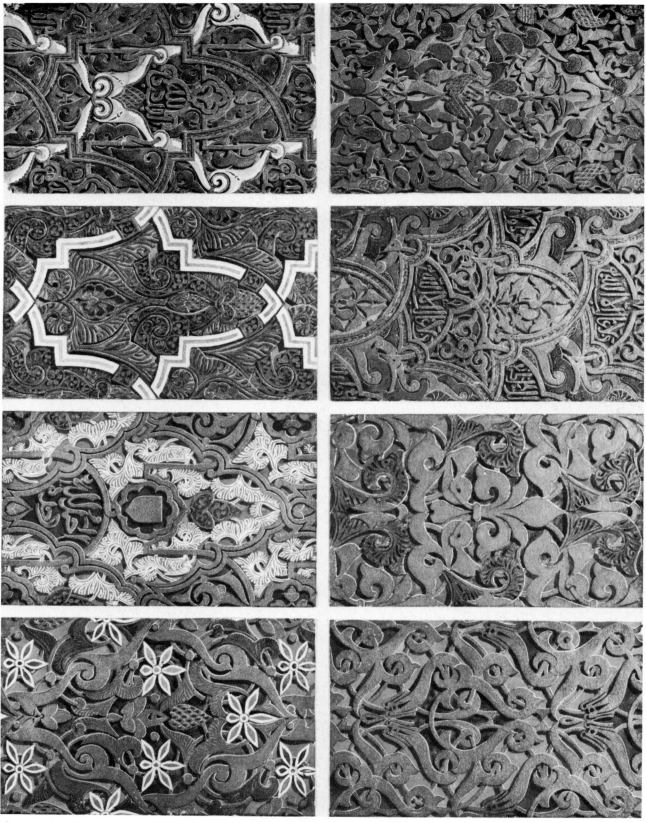

102

103

103 Indian no. 6. Plate LIV.
Drawings (7) cut out and pasted onto a single sheet.
Pencil, pen and ink, water-colour and gold paint. Largest 15 × 31.3.
Victoria and Albert Museum (1627).

The *Grammar of Ornament*, one of the best known and most influential pattern books to be published in the 19th century, appears to have been conceived by Henry Cole and Owen Jones as a means of making the objects in the Museum at Marlborough House, and the principles they embodied, more generally available. In particular Cole and Jones must have had in mind the students in the provincial Schools of Design for whom London was difficult of access. The title emphasises the book's educational role, and it was the Schools which the Department of Art had been set up to administer. Certainly Cole was involved with the *Grammar* at an early date, for he recorded in his diary on 16 February 1852 'O. Jones comes with his materials for Grammar of Ornament.'

The *Grammar* was published in parts throughout 1856 and the early months of 1857. In preparing the text and plates Jones drew freely on the help of his friends including Joseph Bonomi, who provided the material for the Egyptian ornament, and James Wild whose drawings of Cairo were used for the illustrations of Arabian details. James Waring and Matthew Digby Wyatt each contributed a chapter, and Albert Henry Warren and Charles Aubert,

118

together with Mr Stubbs helped to gather the material and draw the plates. Christopher Dresser, then a student at Marlborough House, provided the illustrations of 'leaves and flowers from nature'. As one might have expected, given the need to reflect the nature of the objects in the Museum, no fewer than five out of the twenty chapters are devoted to Islamic ornament, an extraordinarily high proportion.

DRESSER, Christopher (1834-1904)

104 Indian knife and sheath. c.1852.
Signed *C.Dresser.*
Pencil, pen and ink, water-colour, and silver paint. 29.2 × 21.1.
Victoria and Albert Museum (979).

105 Ornament in the Arabian style, intended to be painted in the centre of a ceiling.
Plate XIII, C. Dresser, *Studies in Design*, 1875-76.
Chromolithograph. Page size 30 × 42.4.
Victoria and Albert Museum: National Art Library.

106 Soup tureen and ladle. Manufactured by Hukin and Heath, Birmingham and London, c.1880.
Electroplated; the handles ebony.
Victoria and Albert Museum (M.26 to b-1972).

Although he was born in Glasgow, Christopher Dresser early moved to London where he is recorded to have been a pupil at the School of Design at Somerset House in 1847. In 1852 he won a scholarship to study at Marlborough House, when he presumably heard Owen Jones's four lectures on The True and the False in the Decorative Arts, for in 1853 his scholarship was renewed and he won a prize of £2 for 'applying the principles taught by the Department to a chintz'. It was shortly after this that he supplied the plate illustrating 'principled' plant design to Owen Jones for the *Grammar of Ornament* (1856).

Throughout his life Dresser continued to refer to the work of Jones, and he was clearly very much influenced by him. When Jones died in 1874 Dresser bought a number of drawings at the sale of his effects; and when Dresser took over the Art Editorship of the *Furniture Gazette* in 1880 he began by printing in full the first thirteen of Jones's Principles of Decorative Art, and by reproducing a design by Jones as his first illustration. Dresser considered that Jones's 'skill as an ornamentist surpasses that of any other with whom we are acquainted', and in 1862 he wrote of some of Jones's London buildings 'the excellency of these works calls loudly to us as a nation to do honour to Mr Owen Jones, who created them. I would that the nation should use him more while they have him; when it is too late we shall mourn our folly.'

Not only is Dresser's debt to Jones apparent in many of his designs but also in his writings. The title and phrasing of the *Principles of Decorative Design* (1873), for example, are cribbed from Jones, and like Jones he stressed in all his writings that the ultimate goal of ornamentation should be to produce 'repose'.

Given the extent of his debt to Jones it is not surprising that Dresser advocated the study of

104

106

105

Islamic design. He sought to produce a new ornament which would include the 'richness of the Arabian' and ' the intricacy of plot of the Moorish'. Several of the plates in his *Studies in Design*, 'prepared ... with the hope of assisting to bring about a better style of decoration for our houses', which was published in twenty parts between 1874 and 1876 reveal this. Dresser had studied Islamic ornament himself in detail and advised the student designer to do the same: 'I would also advise the learner to take one or two small portions of the Alhambraic ornament, then one or two small portions of Arabian ornament, then of Turkish, then of Persian; and ... notice carefully the resemblances and differences ... and thus make himself master of the characteristic qualities of each.' As Director of the Art Furnisher's Alliance he encouraged Chubbs, the firm of safe manufacturers to reproduce some Moorish door knockers 'forwarded to Dr Dresser by an assistant whom he sent to Spain and Morocco to make drawings and photographs of all kinds of Moorish remains.' Of the Alhambra itself, he stated in the *Art of Decorative Design*: 'as a decorative scheme it ... is in our judgement much higher than the Vatican, for in the latter the *ornament* is bad and the general effect seems sacrificed to the exceeding power of the pictorial works.'

In the work of Christopher Dresser, who has been described as 'the only true designer for Industry' produced by the Schools of Design in the middle of the last century, one can perhaps see the ultimate expression of the principles advocated by Jones and Cole in the *Grammar of Ornament*. Although it seems rather far fetched to suggest that Dresser's extraordinarily advanced silver designs, which are among the most assertively '20th century' of all 19th century objects, owe something to the Islamic teaching of Jones, the possibility can not be dismissed.

The dagger depicted in Dresser's drawing appears to be one in the Victoria and Albert Museum (2552 IS), which was transferred from the Indian Museum in 1880, and is attributed to Coorg.

Lit. *Christopher Dresser 1834-1904*, Catalogue of the exhibition shown at the Camden Arts Centre and elsewhere, 1979.

SECTION 4

ISLAMIC ARCHITECTURE ABSORBED

Disciplined ornament such as that which Owen Jones and the Departments of Practical Art, and Science and Art, advocated in the 1850s was undoubtedly adopted by many manufacturers in the second half of the century. Matthew Digby Wyatt's views on the acceptance of Oriental patterns were cited at the end of the last section, and a perusal of the vast numbers of designs for textiles, wallpapers, carpets and other two-dimensional objects registered at the Design Registry of the Patent Office suggests that there is some truth in this contention. The precise degree of influence is, however, difficult to measure empirically, partly because 'principled' ornament is not always immediately recognisable as such, and did not automatically engender a style of its own, but also because much 'good' ornamental design was produced quite independently of any Government attempts at improvement. There is some evidence to suggest that the principles simply encouraged some designers to fall back upon specific historical examples which were 'safe', rather than to attempt to design new ornament of their own. The *Grammar of Ornament* too, tended to encourage this attitude, and even today is used by designers as a store of patterns rather than as an educational tool: there has been more than one range of 'Persian' carpeting on the market in recent years which has owed its appearance directly to the plates in this volume.

Although Islamic architecture and decoration continued to influence design in the second half of the century, there was a strong reaction against it too. Jones's work, and that of his circle balances on the fine edge which separates the sublime from the monstrous, and was seen by some contemporaries to topple over on the wrong side. Ruskin, for example, thought the ornamentation of the Alhambra 'detestable ... it is a late building, a work of the Spanish dynasty in its last decline, and its ornamentation is fit for nothing but to be transferred to patterns of carpets or bindings of books, together with their marbling and mottling, and other mechanical recommendations.'[1] He classed 'mechanically drawn patterns of dress, Alhambras and common Moorish ornament ... under the head of "Doggerel ornamentation",[2] and thought that Wild's Christ Church at Streatham, one of his local

churches, was 'spoiled by many grievous errors (the ironwork in the campanile [an Islamic fretwork design] being the grossest)'. Such work was not art and, therefore, could not be taken seriously, although Ruskin did admit to admiring 'the inventive power of the Arab', and did not disapprove of Islamic architecture in general. It was, apparently, Jones's particular expression of it that he could not tolerate. Richard Phené Spiers felt the same: 'I confess, however, that this exuberant richness of design, in the plaster work and painted decoration of the Alhambra, palls upon me, and an inspection of Owen Jones's work on the *Alhambra* and the magnificent court he designed and erected at the Crystal Palace causes me to turn with relief to the simpler but more real decoration in stone, marble and tiles, which is found in Egypt and Constantinople.'[4] 'Real' ornament, inspired by nature and the human figure, developed as an alternative to the teachings of Jones and his circle; and the textile and wallpaper designs of William Morris, and the 'Renaissance' buildings of the Department of Science and Art in the 1860s, embodying the figurative work of many of Alfred Stevens's pupils, have already been cited as examples.

In one sense, then, buildings and designs of the later 19th century in obviously Islamic styles can be said to parallel those reviewed in the first section of this exhibition. None appears to have embodied the radical concepts and serious purpose of those of the mid century by Jones and his circle. Cuthbert Brodrick's Turkish Baths in Leeds, for example, (no. 110) or W. Potter's similar establishment in Manchester, the subject of his *The Roman or Turkish Bath Its Hygienic and Curative Properties* (1859), are surely part of the tradition which was started in the 17th century. Similarly, George Somers Clarke's 'Hammam', opened in Jermyn Street in 1862, perhaps the best known of all Turkish Baths, although meticulously detailed and authentically equipped − it was described by contemporaries as 'the one perfect Turkish Bath in London' − also belongs to this tradition.[5] The fretwork designs in the roof, 'Moorish' doorways, 'Eastern indented lintels', and other Islamic features were dictated by the nature of the building and not

122

by any earnest wish to promote a genuinely new style of architecture.

As far as many of the 'Islamic' buildings which the British erected abroad were concerned, the use of Moorish and other features was motivated in part by a wish not to break with local traditions and introduce new styles. Although, as Gavin Stamp pointed out in a recent lecture about British architecture in India, there was always one faction who believed that conquerors should take their national style with them, as the Muslims had done themselves.[6] Charles Mant's Palace designs (no. 112) are typical of the numerous buildings erected there and elsewhere with Islamic influence. Others which may be cited are: William Emerson's University of Allahabad, which was in course of erection in 1862; Frederick William Stevens's extraordinary designs for Bombay: the Municipal Buildings of 1888-93 and the Church Gate Station for the Bombay, Baroda and Central Indian Railway of 1894-6, for example; Robert Fellows Chisholm's Madras University Senate House and Chepauk Palace, both built in the 1870s; Col. Sir Swinton Jacob's many buildings in Lucknow; John Begg's Bombay Central Post Office of 1903-09; the enormous Law Courts in Madras of 1888-92 by J.W. Brassington, and a host of others, culminating in the New Delhi Government buildings by Sir Edwin Lutyens, from 1912. Ironically, the use of the Islamic style in India perpetuated a form of building evolved by the Mughal dynasty which British rule replaced in 1858 and has provided the inspiration for much modern Indian architecture.

In 1864 John Pollard Seddon's partner John Prichard built a mansion for Senor Don Manuel M. Gonzalez at Jerez de la Frontera in southern Spain which the Building News described as, 'a sort of Mooresque-Gothic'.[7] Many of the Indian buildings listed above are versions of Gothic revival architecture given an Islamic flavour by the introduction of suitable detailing. Some elements of Venetian Gothic architecture in particular were not dissimilar from those which appear in many Islamic buildings – patterned brickwork and striped voussoirs, for example – and consequently the two styles could be integrated quite easily. Byzantine architecture, too, was readily assimilated with Islamic. Indeed, one had strongly influenced the other, and S. Sophia in Constantinople and many other Byzantine buildings in the Near East inherited by the Muslims showed evidence of how the two styles could be integrated. Thus, James Wild's St. Mark's Church in Alexandria of 1848-55, and even John Bentley's, much later, Westminster Cathedral in London, both of which were considered by their architects to be Byzantine, also show some evidence of Islamic influence. At Teheran James Wild's buildings for the British Legation of c.1869 show the application of the style to what appears to be essentially Italianate forms. The combination is managed with more difficulty, and the result, like Edward Blore's 'Aloupka', built as early as 1837 for Prince Woronzow, in the Crimea, is much less picturesque.

The increasing amount of building carried out by the British abroad as a result of the growth of the Empire inevitably had a reciprocal effect on architecture at home, and more works with Islamic influence were carried out during the second half of the nineteenth century than at any other time. Some were the result of a wish to perpetuate the memory of exotic travels, the Moorish smoking room at Rhinefield House, Hampshire, for example, which was commissioned by Mrs L.W. Munro as a reminder of her honeymoon in 1888. Others were designed to incorporate precious objects acquired during travels in the Near East, like the Arab Hall at Leighton House by George Aitchison (no. 113). Many were carried out simply because it was fashionable; the Moorish billiard room at Breadsall Priory, near Derby, designed by Robert Scrivener for Francis Morley in 1861; the Moorish sitting room at Rolleston Hall, Staffordshire, designed by S.J. Waring and Son and demolished in 1926 or the ready-made rooms in Arabic styles advertised by at least one company in the 1890s,[8] might be placed in this category. Yet others were designed in Islamic styles because it was appropriate; H.C. Cole's scheme for an Indian Museum at Knebworth for the Earl of Lytton, which was not carried out, for example, or Matthew Digby Wyatt's India Museum, which has already been mentioned. At least one interior was designed in the Indian Style in order to make its occupant feel at home, that at Elveden Hall, carried out by John Norton (no. 111). Still others cannot be conveniently fitted into any category; the Durbar Hall at Osborne designed by Lockyard Kipling, Rudyard's father and former Professor of Architectural Sculpture at the Bombay School of Art, with Bai Rham Singh in 1890; William Burges's Arab Hall at Cardiff (no. 114); the Turkish room at Sledmere House, Yorkshire, designed by David Ohanessian for Sir Mark Sykes, the statesman and soldier, who had spent a considerable part of his life in the Near East; Lord Brassey's Arab Hall (no. 115); and many, many more.

Oriental influence was not only felt in architecture but also in the applied arts, and numerous items in Islamic styles were produced throughout the second half of the century, quite independently of those designed by Owen Jones and his circle. Matthew Digby Wyatt's Industrial Arts of the Nineteenth Century (1853) and J.B. Waring's equally comprehensive compendium Masterpieces of Industrial Art and Sculpture (1863), illustrate many which were shown at the International Exhibitions of 1851 and 1862, and the volume increased as the century progressed. A growing preoccupation with the Near East also manifested itself in other areas. The Oriental Club, which had been founded in c.1824, could boast more members in 1889 than at any time previously; the number of publications by the Oriental Translation Fund of Great Britain and Ireland, established in 1828, increased markedly; and the Oriental and Turkish Museum moved from its old premises in Leicester Square to new and larger quarters at the St George's Gallery, Hyde Park Corner, in 1854.

In America, too, interest in the Near East and in Islamic decoration was also much in evidence in the second half of the century. Few Americans had been to the Near East, and most learned about it from European publications. John Maas, in *The Victorian Home In America* (1972), notes that by the 1880s: 'even middle-class Americans could afford a "Turkish corner"' in one of their rooms, and that 'many homes sported some Moorish details'. He quotes from the advertisement of one mail order firm who offered advice about the Moorish style in the 1890s with the promise that 'a little taste combined with judicious expenditure can transform a room into a palace.' Of entire buildings in the Islamic style the Horticultural Hall of the Philadelphia Centennial Exhibition of 1876 by Hermann J. Schwarzman, 'an enchanted palace of iron, glass and colored bricks', described as being in the Saracenic style but in fact a mixture of Indian and Alhambresque; and Olana, the house built by the Hudson River School painter, Frederick Church, to the designs of Calvert Vaux, one of Jacob Wrey Mould's collaborators in the development of Central Park in New York (no. 66), must surely rank among the most interesting. Olana survives, but the Horticultural Hall was demolished as recently as 1955. Another extraordinary 'Islamic' house which still survives is 'Longwood' which the Philadelphia architect Samuel Sloan designed for the cotton planter Haller Nutt at Natchez, Mississippi. Octagonal in form with a central dome, Sloan may have been influenced by the Dome of the Rock in Jerusalem. He illustrated it as an 'Oriental Villa' in his *Homestead Architecture* (1861) noticing that: 'fancy dictated that the dome should be bulbiform – a remembrancer of Eastern magnificence which few will judge misplaced as it looms up against the mellowed azure of a southern sky.' As for largest 'Islamic' building in the United States, that must surely be the Tampa Bay Hotel, now the University of Tampa, in Florida, which was built in the 1880s.

Clearly it is not possible to do justice to this multiplicity of buildings and objects in one small section of an exhibition of this size. It is hoped, however, that the designs which are displayed will give some impression of the breadth and variety of Islamic influence in the second half of the century, and provide a prologue, so to speak, to the earlier work with which this exhibition is chiefly concerned.

Notes

1 *Complete Works*, IX, 1904, p. 469.
2 *Ibid.*, IV, 1904, p. 333.
3 *Ibid.*, IX, 1904, p. 349.
4 R. Phené Spiers, *Architecture East and West*, 1905, p. 23.
5 *Building News*, 4 July 1862, p. 12.
6 Reprinted in *Journal* of the Royal Society of Arts, CXXIX, May 1981, pp. 357-379.
7 *Building News*, 6 May 1864, p. 333.
8 Illustrated in E. Aslin, *Nineteenth Century Furniture*, 1962, pl. 106.

LEWIS, Thomas Hayter (1818-1898)

107 The Royal Panopticon, Leicester Square, London. 1852.
Illustration in the *Illustrated London News*, 31 January 1852, p. 96.
Photograph.

108 Interior view of the Royal Panopticon. 1854.
Illustration in the *Builder*, 18 March 1854, p. 143.
Photograph.

On 21 February 1850 a royal charter was granted to Edward Marmaduke Clarke and the other shareholders in a company set up to build the Royal Panopticon 'an institution for scientific exhibitions, and for promoting discoveries in arts and manufactures'. By October 1851 they had been granted a lease of 66 years on the site on the east side of Leicester Square, and building began shortly

THE ROYAL PANOPTICON, LEICESTER-SQUARE.

107

108

after. The Panopticon was completed by 16 March 1854 when it was opened. In spite of daily attendances in excess of 1000, however, the enterprise was a failure, resulting, as one writer put it: 'from the unnatural alliance ... of religious profession and commercial enterprize'. In August 1856 the premises were put up for sale, and were bought by E.T. Smith for £9,000 (the estimated cost of building the Panopticon had been £80,000), and from this time the building became known as the Alhambra, and was used for musical and theatrical performances, until its demolition shortly after 8 October 1936.

The Council of the Royal Panopticon gave considerable thought to the style of their new building, and Clarke chose 'the Saracenic or Moorish' style, 'as a novelty'. Hayter Lewis, the company's architect, objected strongly at first, but eventually accepted it after realising that he 'would obtain a tolerably free scope in working out the design'. In fact, on the exterior at least, the Islamic element of his design consisted of little more than a cladding of polychrome decoration on to what were essentially three terraced house fronts, and the addition of two minarets behind. Much of the decoration was of Minton's tiles and must have struck a strange note in juxtaposition with its sober surroundings. The great glass dome was replaced in execution by a low cone with flat skylight. Inside, the main feature was the Great Hall or rotunda,

described in the *Illustrated Handbook* as: 'the most splendid room ever appropriated to scientific and artistic purposes'. In the centre was a fountain supplied from an artesian well on the premises, and the walls were lined with Derbyshire alabaster and with other decorations in enamelled slate and glass mosaic. Coupled with the elaborate ceiling painting by Harland and Fisher, the effect of all this decoration, much of it designed by Lewis himself, must have been very impressive

Lewis's sources for the decoration are revealed in an article in the *Civil Engineer and Architect's Journal*: 'ordinary houses in the East, which have usually the most simple square-headed windows' were not acceptable for that reason; but, 'a model ... was found by a reference to the buildings of Grand Cairo ... the Mosques of Zalaon and El Moyed in particular, furnish most admirably bold and picturesque outlines and details. These have been copied with such modifications as are rendered necessary by modern European habits.' Lewis made an extended tour abroad in 1841-2, and although it is not certain, it is possible that he visited Cairo at this time. Alternatively, his sources may have been the published drawings and photographs of friends and colleagues such as his partner Thomas Finden, the brother of William Finden the artist, or Edward Clarke himself, the father of C. Purdon Clarke. Whatever the case, Lewis certainly made many trips to the Near East in later life, and gave various

126

109

lectures on Moorish, Persian, Cairene and other facets of Islamic architecture.

Lewis's obituaries record that he became involved in designing a hall for Cairo which was similar to the Panopticon in style, but although he sent complete sets of drawings to the Khedive, it does not appear to have been built.

Lit. Survey of London XXXIV, *The Parish of St. Anne, Soho*, 1966, pp. 492-97.
Builder, 14 May 1853, pp. 308-9.
Civil Engineer and Architect's Journal, XVI, 1853, p. 161.

SPIERS, Richard Phené (1838-1916)

109 Interior of the Great Han, Damascus. 1865.
Water-colour. 25.3 × 35.8.
Searight Collection.

Phené Spiers made a tour in the Near East in 1865-66 as a result of winning the Royal Academy's travelling studentship, and the interest in Islamic architecture which he acquired at this time remained with him for the rest of his life. In 1887 he published a number of his travel drawings as *A Series of 36 Views of Ancient and Modern Egypt*, 'with a short description of each plate'; and in 1905 a series of his essays and lectures were published under the title *Architecture East and West*. These included 'Mahometan Architecture' (a lecture given to the Architectural Association on 3 February 1888); 'Stalactite (Honeycomb) Vaulting, its Origin in Saracenic Architecture' (an article first published in the *Journal* of the Royal Institute of British Architects, 26 April 1888); 'The Great Mosque of the Omeiyades, Damascus' (first published in the same *Journal*, 1896-8, and reprinted in the *Architectural Review*, VIII, 1900); and 'The Influence of Greek Art on the Persian Order' (first published in the *Builder* 11 June 1904). Spiers of necessity derived much of his information from other sources, in particular S. Lane Poole, *The Art of the Saracens in Egypt* (1886) and Guy le Strange, *Palestine under the Moslems: a Description of Syria and the Holy Land from AD 650 to 1500* (1890), so that much of his writing has a text-book quality which befitted his position as Master at the Architectural School at the Royal Academy from 1870 to 1906. In this position he, perhaps more than anyone else, was responsible for introducing young architectural students in the last decades of the century to Islamic architecture. Indeed, it was in token of his work in this respect that his students and others published *Architecture East and West* as part of the Testimonial which was presented to him when he retired.

This particular drawing may have been among those of Damascus which the young W.R. Lethaby, writing about Spiers at the time of his death in 1916, particularly remembered being shown by Spiers after he returned from his travels in 1866.

Lit. *Journal of the Royal Institute of British Architects*, 1916, p. 334.

BRODRICK, Cuthbert (1822-1905)

110 Oriental Baths, Cookridge Street, Leeds. 1866.
Pen and ink, and water-colour. 84.4 × 48.5.
British Architectural Library: Drawings Collection.

The *Builder* noted at the time Cuthbert Brodrick's Corn Exchange at Leeds was completed in 1862: 'Mr Brodrick has done good service by introducing the use of ... moulded brickwork into his King Street Warehouses. Thus, with red, blue and black brick, moulded brick string courses and mouldings, encaustic tiles and terra cotta, we have a stock of materials which no climate will touch or destroy; and with them a field for design, both in form and colour that will give architects opportunities for exercising every artistic facility they possess'. The possibilities that such brightly polychromed, but still permanent materials provided for 'exercising every artistic facility' certainly did not pass Brodrick himself by, for they not only appeared in this design, but also in another of the same date, for the Custom House at Bombay, 'in a mixture of Hindoo and Mohammedan', which was never built. Perhaps it was the use of these materials which suggested exotic designs to Brodrick in the first instance.

The Cookridge Street baths were refaced in the Gothic style, including a swimmer diving out of a niche, in 1882, and demolished in 1969.

Lit. J. Physick and M. Darby, *op. cit.*, p.134, no. 86, and sources cited therein.

NORTON, John (1823-1904)

111 Interior, Elveden Hall, Suffolk. 1871.
Photograph by A.F. Kersting.

Duleep Singh, 'Queen Victoria's Maharajah', acquired Elveden Hall, near Thetford, from William Newton at a cost of some £105,000, which was lent to him by the India Office at 4 per cent. Some time later he bought part of the adjoining estate of Eriswell by which time the total amount of land he owned amounted to some 17,000 acres. Elveden itself was remodelled by John Norton in the Italian Renaissance style from 1869, after the Maharajah had decided to pull down all but two rooms of the earlier house. When the main fabric was complete: 'Mr Norton had the gratification of being instructed to decorate the interior with pure Indian ornament, which he has been able to carry out by the aid of careful models prepared by Messrs Cubitt, and by the study of Bourne's photographs; objects in the India Museum; and details obtained from a collection of native water-colour drawings, brought by the prince from Lahore and elsewhere.' The resulting ornamentation is very lavish, involving inlaid marble floors and chimney pieces; encaustic tiles especially made by Maw and Company; and ceiling and wall panels 'of most minute and

110

elaborate Indian design'. The whole of the painting and gilding was carried out by Mr Holzman, while Powells of Whitefriars made the silvered glass enrichments in the great drawing room.

Elveden was sold in 1894 after Duleep Singh's death to the first Earl of Iveagh for £159,000, and has remained with the family since.

Lit. *Builder*, 18 November 1871, pp. 905-7.
  Architect, 18 March 1871, p. 147.
  M. Alexander and S. Anand, *Queen Victoria's Maharajah Duleep Singh 1838-93*, 1980.

MANT Charles (1848-1881)

112 Design for a palace in India, perhaps at Cooch Behar. c.1875.
Water-colour. 98 × 48.
Victoria and Albert Museum (D.275-1904).

While buildings incorporating Islamic features were erected in Britain exceptionally, in India many British architects adopted the style almost as the rule. Some of their works are mentioned in the Introduction to this section, but these represent only a small proportion of what was built. Throughout the second half of the 19th and into the present century British architects and engineers were involved in a wide range of constructional work in the sub-continent from railways and docks, to schools and palaces. The degree of influence of Mughal building was always greater than Hindoo, and varied from simple iron panels with fretwork designs, like those which ornament Matthew Digby Wyatt and James Rendel's bridge over the River Son, near Patna, of c.1855, to the rich vocabulary of plastic forms used by Sir Edwin Lutyens in building the enormous official residence and government offices at Delhi from 1912.

Charles Mant first went out to India in 1859 as a Royal Engineer and rapidly established a reputation as one of the more brilliant young architects working there. His first buildings, the High School at Surat and the Town Hall at Kolhapur were in the Italian gothic style, but after becoming fascinated by Indian architecture, Mant abandoned this style in order to be able 'to unite the usefulness of the scientific European designs together with the beauty, taste, grandeur and sublimity of the native style'. As a result he became one of the earliest exponents of the 'Indo-Saracenic' style, and designed a large number of schools, halls and other public buildings in it. Mant also produced designs for palaces for the Maharajas of Darbhanga, Baroda and Kolhapur but he did not live to see them completed, the Maharaja of Baroda recalling: 'while all three palaces had simultaneously reached little farther than the foundations, he lost control of his senses, became convinced that his palatial designs would fall down because he had done his sums wrong, and died tragically while still in his forties.'

This design does not appear to relate to those for the palaces mentioned above, but is very similar in plan, if not in style, to that at Cooch Behar built for Nripendra Narain and his wife Sunity Devee (1875-1890) and may be an early scheme for it.

There is a photograph of Mant's design for Rajiram's High School at Kolhapur in the British Architectural Library: Drawings Collection.

Lit. G. Stamp, *op. cit.*, p. 366.
  Building News, 10 May 1872, p. 381.
  Maharaja of Baroda, *The Palaces of India*, 1980, pp. 126-131.

129

111

112

113

AITCHISON, George (1825-1910)

113 Arab Hall, Leighton House, Holland Park Road, Kensington, London. 1877-79.
Signed on the mount *George Aitchison ARA, 150 Harley St. W* and dated *March 1880.* Inscribed *Arab Hall, Kensington W, Sir F. Leighton Bart. PRA.*
Water-colour and gold paint heightened with white. 43.7 × 63.4.
British Architectural Library: Drawings Collection.

Sir Frederick, later Lord Leighton (1830-1896), the painter and sculptor, commissioned his life long friend George Aitchison to design Leighton House in 1866, and subsequently employed him to make various alterations and additions. These were partly inspired by two tours which Leighton had made in the East in 1868 and 1873. After the first, he employed Aitchison to supply designs for the two Arabian windows in the studio, and after the second to design the Arab Hall. Leighton had acquired a large collection of oriental ceramics and other objects while on his tours, including several large tile panels. These presented a storage problem and George Aitchison 'offered to furnish him with a design that would be suited to their employment'. The *Building News* noted that Leighton gave Aitchison *'carte blanche'*, and the result was the Arab Hall, built between 1877 and 1879.

According to Aitchison and Walter Crane the design of the Arab Hall was based on the 12th century Palace of La Zisa in Palermo. Some of the capitals of the columns were modelled by (Sir) J. Edgar Boehm to Aitchison's designs and others partly by Randolph Caldecott. The mosaic frieze was designed by Walter Crane. The builders were Messrs Woodward of Finsbury; Messrs White and Sons executed the extensive marble work; Harland and Fisher the painted decorations; and Burke and Company the mosaics. The Ormonds note that William de Morgan was responsible 'for arranging the tiles in the Arab Hall ... These are mainly Syrian and Isnic ware of the late sixteenth and seventeenth century. Many of the sets were incomplete or did not match, and De Morgan had to do some clever infilling. The patchwork arrangement of the tiles is quite unlike anything one would find in an Arabian domestic interior, or in a mosque ....' Leighton had hoped to continue the mosaic decoration onto the roof but this project fell through. The carved wooden lattice work in the windows and first floor gallery is from Damascus, and dates from the 17th century.

The Arab Hall was well received after completion, Mrs Haweis described it as 'a Moorish dream' in *Beautiful Houses* (1882), and Vernon Lee as 'quite the 8th wonder of the world' when he visited Leighton in 1883. Today it remains perhaps the most successful, and certainly one of the most enjoyable, of all the Islamic interiors which were carried out in this country in the second half of the century.

Lit.   J. Physick and M. Darby, *op. cit.*, p. 90, no. 46.
       Building News, 8 October 1880, p.
       L. and R. Ormond, *Lord Leighton*, 1975.

BURGES, William (1827-1881)

114 The Arab Hall, Cardiff Castle. 1880.
Modern photograph courtesy of *Country Life*.

William Burges's Arab Hall at Cardiff Castle, which he designed for Lord Bute, was building at the same time as Aitchison's Arab Hall for Frederick Leighton. Burges and Aitchison were friends, and it seems likely that it was Aitchison's work at Leighton House, which was begun shortly before that at Cardiff, that may have been the inspiration for Burges's design. Burges may well have harboured the idea of an Islamic room for some time before this, however. As a student of Matthew Digby Wyatt at the time Wyatt was working on the Great Exhibition, Burges came into contact with the circle of Owen Jones at the period of their peak activity. He wrote articles on damascening for Wyatt, and helped with the *Industrial Arts* (1853). He probably also knew Wyatt's work at the India Museum and may well have visited the billiard room at 12 Kensington Palace Gardens (nos. 70, 71). Furthermore, he had visited Constantinople in 1857 as a result of winning the competition for the Crimea Memorial Church, and had studied the mosques there, enjoying their 'breadth and massiveness', noting the disposition of the ornament, and admiring the coloured glass especially. In 1870 he designed a 'kiosque' for Colonel C.H. Luard, and in 1875 he commissioned Axel Haig to travel to Palermo to draw the honeycombed ceilings there (were these the drawings which inspired Aitchison perhaps?).

For the actual details of the Arab Hall Burges turned to A.C.T.E. Prisse d'Avennes, *L'Art Arabe d'aprés les Monuments du Kaire 7e-18e*, which he bought shortly after publication in 1877. Mordaunt Crook notices that the 'stalactite vaults, his honey

114

comb glass, his "meshrebeŷeh" trellis, and his kufic inscriptions, can all be traced to the gilded plates of this exotic publication'. Not everything came from this book, however, the shallow arches with gothic carving in the centre of three of the walls are copied directly from those which John Pollard Seddon designed for Samuel Heard at Rosdohan House in Co. Kerry, Ireland, in 1875-78. 'Suffocating richness' was Burges's aim, notes Mordaunt Crook: 'The dado is lined with Italian dove marble. The upper walls are faced with tiles by Simpson of almost Iznic quality. Wall cabinets are built of cedar wood and mounted in silver. Around the walls Burges inserted niches for statuettes of Eastern gods. And along the fretted cornice he placed eight gilded parrots flanked by glittering crystals. The windows can be shuttered into pinpoints of light. Above the fireplace, mosaic and lapis lazuli glitter in a sea of milky marble. And as for the stained glass: "sliced jewels".'

The Arab room like the study, which is also situated in the Herbert Tower, was among the last which Burges designed. There are drawings for it in Cardiff dated 26 March 1881, only two days before his last visit to the castle and three weeks before his death on 20 April. Subsequently, Bute inscribed the chimney piece in the room as his memorial.

Lit. J. Mordaunt Crook, *William Burges and the High Victorian Dream*, 1981.
  Seddon's work at Rosdohan is illustrated in the *Architect*, 26 March 1881, p. 219.

115 The Durbar Hall, 24 Park Lane, London. c.1880.
19th century photograph. 27.5 × 21.4.
Hastings Museum and Art Gallery.

116 The Smoking Room, Rhinefield House, Hampshire. c.1890.
Modern photograph.

These interiors have been selected as examples of the work of foreign artists in Britain. The Durbar Hall, erected by the first Lord Brassey at his home at 24 Park Lane, London, originally formed part of the Indian display at the Colonial and Indian Exhibition held in London in 1886. It was built by Muhammed

115

Baksh and Muhammed Juma, two natives of Bhera in the Punjab, who were brought to England in 1885 to do the carved work which occupied them for nine months. Their names are inscribed on a panel in the room. Lord Brassey had been one of the Commissioners for the exhibition and acquired the room after it closed in order to form a museum for the extensive collections of ethnographic and other material made by his wife while travelling on their yacht the *Sunbeam* between 1876 and 1883. In fact, Brassey's penchant for Eastern design goes back at least as early as the late 1860s when he employed Owen Jones to decorate the ceilings of several rooms at 24 Park Lane.

In 1919 the second Earl Brassey presented the Hall to the Borough of Hastings. It was carefully taken down under the supervision of Professor Stanley Adshead, and re-erected as an annexe to the Hastings museum, where it still survives. The room was formally opened there on 29 April 1932.

The Moorish smoking room at Rhinefield Hall, a large house in the New Forest designed in the Elizabethan style by Romaine Walker and Tanner, for Lionel Walker Munroe, in 1889-90, also survives. Walker Munroe was a lieutenant in the Royal Navy, and the story goes that his wife, previously Miss Walker of Barber and Walker, the Nottinghamshire colliery owners, had the smoking room built as a surprise present for her husband while he was out of the country. A somewhat similar, although less elaborate 'Turkish' room was designed for Sir Mark Sykes, the eminent orientalist, at his home Sledmere House in Yorkshire, by the Armenian artist David Ohanessian, who is said to have copied one of the Sultan's apartments in the Valideh Mosque, Istanbul. The tiles for this room were made in Damascus.

Lit. J. Manwaring Baines, *The Durbar Hall and the Brassey Collections*, Hastings, n.d. (c.1936).
Builder 9 May 1874, p. 385; 17 August 1889, pp. 121-2.
M. Girouard, *The Victorian Country House*, 1971, pp. 26, 186.
Guide book to Sledmere House.

117 Four postcard views by Valentine and Sons, Ltd., of the Court of Honour, Franco-British Exhibition, London. 1908.
Colour photographs. Each 19 × 13.9.
Private Collection.

Perhaps no more grandiose Islamic experience was ever contrived for the inhabitants of London than the Court of Honour in the Franco-British Exhibition, better known as the White City, of 1908. The buildings, made primarily of plaster, were designed by Imre Kiralfy, the prime mover and mastermind of the whole enterprise. Born in Budapest in 1849, Kiralfy exhibited considerable talent as a singer at an early age and was presented as an infant prodigy to Frederick William IV of Prussia. Later, he took up conjuring and became a favourite of Archduke Maximilian. At the age of 12 he became interested in civil and automotive engineering and built a car. Music continued to fascinate him, however, and after organising various musical fêtes in Paris and Brussels, he travelled to the United States in 1869. There he was responsible, amongst other things, for putting on a production of 'Nero or the Burning of Rome' which involved a cast of 1,500 performers and a specially built stage on Staten Island with a proscenium opening 485 ft wide. He moved to London in the early 1890s with a production of 'Venice in London', and later became Director of Earls Court which was built to his plans.

Kiralfy conceived the White City one night while lying awake in bed 'as if by magic, I saw, stretched out in my mind's eye, an imposing city of palaces, domes and towers, set in cool green spaces and intersected by many bridged canals ... this city was spotlessly white. I saw it all in an instant, and the next day I had jotted down the scheme.' This must have been some time before 18 February 1905 when *The Graphic* reproduced the first published views of the proposal. In fact Kiralfy's vision was almost certainly much influenced by the Chicago Exhibition of 1893 with its many elaborate white plaster buildings, and his detailing of the Court of Honour, originally designed as the Indian Court, by the buildings at Amritsar in India.

The Exhibition opened in the pouring rain on 14 May 1908 and was hailed as a great success, particularly in its promotion of a new 'entente cordiale' between Britain and France. It closed on 31 October 1908. Now all that survives is the famous stadium, one of the largest and most interesting of its day, and the setting for the 1908 Olympic Games, and the entrance on Shepherd's Bush Green to what was intended to be a raised railway which would whisk passengers above ground to the exhibition, but which remained simply an elevated walkway.

Lit. Volume of press cuttings in Hammersmith Central Library.
Information in the possession of the author.

116

In Court of Honour, Franco-British Exhibition, London, 1908

117

SECTION 5

BIOGRAPHIES

AITCHISON, George (1825-1910)

Son of an architect of the same name to whom he was articled after leaving Merchant Taylors School. Studied at the Royal Academy Schools and at London University. After travelling with William Burges on the Continent, where he met Frederick Leighton and Alfred Waterhouse, he became his father's partner in 1859. When the latter died in 1861 he succeeded him as architect to the St Katherine's Dock Company. His work included warehouses and wharves on the Thames; offices at 59-61 Mark Lane; Leighton House, Holland Park Road, London; and numerous interior decorative schemes including the Goldsmiths' Hall and the Founders' Hall. Drawings for many of these works were presented to the Royal Institute of British Architects by his executors in 1910. He was President of the Architects' Benevolent Society 1897-8; Professor of Architecture at the Royal Academy 1887-1905; Fellow of the Royal Institute of British Architects 1862 and subsequently elected Vice President (1889-1893) and President (1896-99). He was awarded the Royal Gold Medal of the Institute in 1898. He was also a member of several foreign architectural bodies, and won a number of medals for overseas architectural competitions.

ALLOM, Thomas (1804-1872)

Born in London on 13 March 1804. Articled to Francis Goodwin, the architect, and remained with him for almost eight years, during which time he worked on many important public and private buildings, and attended classes at the Royal Academy. Allom became as much an artist as an architect and travelled extensively on the Continent and in the Near East to prepare the illustrations for many topographical books. He also made drawings for other architects, including the views of the Houses of Parliament which Charles Barry presented to the Czar of Russia in 1843. His main architectural works were the Church of St Peter, Kensington Park Road, Paddington, London (1852), the Town Hall, Harwich, Essex, built as the Great Eastern Hotel (1864), and the hotel at Lords Cricket Ground, St John's Wood, London. He also designed the Dodd Mausoleum in Norwood Cemetery, and several of the interiors at Highclere Castle. He died on 21 October at his residence in Barnes, London.

Two large water-colour drawings by Allom of Designs for the Thames Embankments are in the Victoria and Albert Museum bequeathed by his daughter Mrs Amy Giovanna Storr.

ARUNDALE, Francis Vyvyan Jago (1807-1853)

Born in London on 9 August 1807. Became a pupil of Augustus Pugin with whom he remained for seven years. During this time he executed some of the plates for the *Public Buildings of London* (1825-28), which Pugin wrote with John Britton, and perhaps met W.H. Bartlett. Later, he accompanied Pugin on the Continent and assisted him with the *Architectural Antiquities of Normandy* (1828). Admitted to the royal Academy schools 22 April 1829 but soon moved to Rome where he spent some time drawing antiquities. He then travelled to Egypt to join Robert Hay's expedition and remained in the Near East for nine years before travelling home via Greece, Sicily, Italy and France. In spite of his training Arundale does not seem to have practised as an architect. The only building known to have been designed by him was a boat house for Charles Bowyer Adderly at Ham's Hall, Warwicks., the design of which he showed at the Royal Academy in 1839. (This is probably the same boat house for which there are drawings in the Griffith Institute, Oxford.) He did publish two volumes of architectural drawings, however: a selection of Palladio's 'most admired buildings from drawings and measurements taken at Vicenza', under the title *The Edifices of A. Palladio* (1832), and a volume of twenty-six *Examples and Designs of Verandahs* (1851).

Arundale was probably best known as an artist. He exhibited some forty-three works at the Royal Academy and British Institution, and married the daughter of H.W. Pickersgill, herself a distinguished miniaturist. He died in Brighton on 9 September 1853. There is a pencil portrait of him by Brockenden in the National Portrait Gallery (2515:36).

BARTLETT, William Henry (1809-1854)

Born in Kentish Town, London, on 26 March 1809. In 1823 he was articled to John Britton, the architect, and executed the drawings for Britton's *Cathedral Antiquities of Great Britain* (1814-1835) and *Picturesque Antiquities of Old Cities* (1828-30). The journeys abroad which were to occupy most of the rest of his life began almost immediately after his marriage on 6 July 1831 to Miss Susannah Moon, niece of the future Lord Mayor of London (for whom Owen Jones designed a 'Moorish' house) when he travelled in Holland and up the Rhine. Apart from the visits he made to the Near East, he also travelled four times to the United States of America and Canada (between 1836 and 1852) in order to make the drawings for his *American Scenery* (1840) and *Canadian Scenery* (1842).

Bartlett died on board the French steamer *Egyptus* on his homeward voyage from the East between Malta and Marseilles on 13 September 1854, and was buried at sea. His drawings were sold at auction by Southgate and Barrett in the following year.

BONOMI, Joseph (1796-1878)

Born in Rome on 9 October 1796, the son of Joseph Bonomi, the architect. Moved with his father to London shortly after. Studied as a sculptor at the Royal Academy and as a pupil of Nollekens. Revisited Rome in 1823, and in the following year accompanied Robert Hay to Egypt. He remained there eight years studying and drawing ancient monuments, in company with Burton, Lane and Wilkinson. In 1833 he joined Catherwood and Arundale on their visit to Sinai and the Holy Land. On his return to England he was much employed illustrating the Egyptological works of Wilkinson and Birch, before, in 1842, he and James Wild joined Lepsius's expedition to Egypt. On his return after an absence of two years he made a series of drawings from which Henry Warren and James Fahey painted their *Panorama of the Nile* which was popular in London and several other large towns. In 1853 he assisted Owen Jones with the Egyptian Court at the Crystal Palace at Sydenham in which he erected full-size copies of the figures at Abu Simbel.

Bonomi's skill as an artist and hieroglyphic draughtsman ensured that he was much employed by Egyptian scholars, and his illustrations are to be found in most of the more important works of the day. He also continued to practise as a sculptor exhibiting works at the Royal Academy and at the Crystal Palace at Sydenham. Although he was not a scholar in the sense of many of his contemporaries, he was a useful contributor to the *Transactions of the Royal Society of Literature* and other learned periodicals.

CARTER, Owen Browne (1806-1859)

Lived for most of his life in Winchester where he had a large architectural practice. Travelled to Egypt to join Robert Hay's expedition down the Nile in 1829. When the Archaeological Institute visited Winchester in 1845 he acted as one of the Secretaries for the architectural section, and read a paper on the Church of East Meon, Hampshire, which he illustrated with his own drawings. He exhibited four architectural drawings at the Royal Academy between 1847 and 1851, and published illustrations in a number of books of local interest, including P. Hall, *Picturesque Memorials of Winchester* (1830), and in Weale's *Quarterly Papers on Architecture*. In 1841 he published four *Picturesque Views in and near Basingstoke*, and drawings exist in the Wiltshire Archaeological Society for a work on Wiltshire churches, only a few numbers of which were ever published. Carter's architectural work included churches at Otterbourne, Hants. (1837-9); Ampfield, Hants. (1838-40); Colemore, Hants. (1845); and Nutley, Hants. (1846); all in the Gothic style, and the Corn Exchange at Winchester, described by H. Colvin as 'an attractive and effective' classical design.

CATHERWOOD, Frederick (1799-1854)

Born in Hoxton, London in 1799. Apprenticed in 1815 to Michael Meredith, the architect, and made a tour of England with him. In 1820, under the guidance of his friend Joseph Severn, attended the free architectural lectures at the Royal Academy. Travelled to Rome in September 1821 to join Severn. Met there Joseph Bonomi. Subsequently travelled with J.J. Scoles and T.L. Donaldson to Greece, and thence to Egypt where he made a journey down the Nile in company with Scoles, Henry Parke and Henry Westcar. It was reputedly study of the drawings which Catherwood and Parke made on this trip that finally persuaded Robert Hay to mount his first Egyptian expedition in 1824. In 1828 Catherwood accompanied Hay on his second expedition. After leaving Hay in 1832 Catherwood undertook some engineering work for Mohammed Ali including the repair of mosques in Cairo. He then visited Sinai and Palestine with Francis Arundale and Joseph Bonomi before returning to London in 1835 and setting up his drawings of Jerusalem as a panorama in Leicester Square. It was during a showing of this Panorama that Catherwood first met John Lloyd Stephens with whom he made two journeys to Central America to study Mayan architecture in 1839 and 1841. Stephens's well known *Incidents of Travel in Central America, Chiapas and Yucatan* (1841) and *Incidents of Travel in Yucatan* (1843) record their adventures and are illustrated with Catherwood's drawings. Subsequently Catherwood published his own *Views of Ancient Monuments in Central America* (1844) employing Owen Jones as printer and publisher, and Henry Warren, George Moore and other artists to make the drawings on stone. From November 1845 he acted as engineer to various railway companies in Central and Southern America. He died on board the SS *Arctic* on 29 September 1854 when it sank after a collision on a journey to North America.

COSTE, Pascal Xavier (1787-1879)

Born in Marseilles on 28 November 1787. Student of the architects Penchaud and J.B.A. Labadye, and of the Ecole des Beaux Arts. Travelled in Egypt in 1818 when he was employed by Mohammed Ali to construct various canals and to re-organise the defences of Aboukir. In 1828 he returned to France and set up as an architect in Marseilles. Shortly afterwards he won first prize, with Barral, for the Church of St Lazare at Marseilles, which was executed between 1833 and 1837. Subsequently they also built the churches of St Joseph, St Barnabas (1845) and another at Mazargues (1847). Between 1854-60 he erected the Exchange in Marseilles with Ferrie. Coste published a detailed autobiography in 1878 entitled *Mémoires d'un Artiste. Notes et Souvenirs de Voyages (1817-1877)*.

GOURY, Jules (1803-1834)

Born in Landerneau, Brittany and studied architecture in Paris under Leclere. Embarked on a Grand Tour in 1830, and by 1832 was in Greece with the German architect Gottfried Semper, studying classical temples. In a footnote in his *Die vier Elemente der Baukunst* (1851), Semper praised Goury, as 'this excellent artist, strong in mind and body, whose energy and ability was equal to his talent.' In the same work Semper also noticed that he and Goury separated in Athens and that 'Goury together with Mr Owen Jones ... continued his researches in Egypt and Syria'. Subsequently Jones and Goury travelled to Turkey and thence to Granada, where Goury died of cholera on 28 August 1834.

HARVEY, William (1796-1866)

Born at Newcastle-upon-Tyne on 13 July 1796. At the age of fourteen was apprenticed to Thomas Bewick with whom he became a great favourite. Moved to London in September 1817 to study drawing under Haydn and anatomy under Sir Charles Bell. During this time he executed Haydn's 'Assassination of Dentatus', probably the most ambitious wood engraving to have been cut in this country at that date. After the death in 1822 of John Thurston, the chief designer of wood engravings in London, Harvey gave up engraving in order to do more designing, and speedily established a good reputation for work on both copper and wood. By 1839 a writer in the *Art Union* recorded that 'the history of wood engraving for some years past, is almost a record of the works of his [Harvey's] pencil'. He is recorded to have been an amiable, unpretending man, 'although he grew with time unpleasantly mannered'. He died at his home Prospect Lodge, Richmond Park, on 13 January 1866, the last of Bewick's surviving pupils.

HAY, Robert (1799-1863)

Born 6 January 1799 at Duns Castle, Berwickshire, the tenth child of Robert Hay of Drumelzien and Whittingehame. Entered Royal Navy in 1812. Visited the Near East for the first time while serving on HMS *Wasp* in 1818. Surviving journals indicate that he had already acquired a taste for antiquarian and archaeological work by this date. May have accompanied Hyett, Vivian and Dupré on their tour in the Balkans in the early part of 1819. Later in this year he travelled to South America, returning in 1820 after he inherited the estate of Linplum following his brother James's death. With his newly acquired wealth financed the two expeditions to Egypt with which his name is most often associated. The first took place from 1824 to 1828, and the second from 1829 to 1834. On both expeditions he hired artists to make detailed studies of the ancient monuments on the banks of the Nile. They included Joseph Bonomi, Frederick Catherwood, Owen Carter, Francis Arundale, Edward Lane and Charles Laver.

Hay married Kalitza Psaraki, the daughter of the chief magistrate of Apodhulo, Crete, in Malta on 19 May 1828; and after completing the second of his Egyptian expeditions settled with her and their children in Scotland. He experienced financial problems in the management of his estates, however, and in 1850 moved with his family to the Continent. They remained there some time, principally in Germany and Italy, before returning again to Scotland. Hay died at Amisfield House on 4 November 1863. His collections of antiquities and drawings are now in the British Museum, where the latter occupy forty-nine volumes.

JONES, Owen (1809-1874)

Born in Thames Street, London, the son of Owain Myfyr, a Welsh furrier and author of the *Myvyrian Archaiology of Wales*. Educated at Charterhouse School. Became a pupil of the architect Lewis Vulliamy, and for a short time of the surveyor William Wallen. Attended classes at the Royal Academy. Travelled on the Continent and in the Near East 1830-1833. On returning to London he set up both as a colour printer and as an architect. His buildings, most of which have now been demolished, included two houses in Kensington Palace Gardens for J.M. Blashfield (1843-47); decoration of the Crystal Palace (1851); St. James's Concert Hall (1856); the Crystal Palace Bazaar (1857); Osler's Gallery, Oxford Street, London (1858) and numerous decorative works. He prepared designs for large iron and glass buildings at Muswell Hill, London, and St Cloud, Paris, which were not carried out, and entered several competitions including Birmingham Town Hall (1830); Army and Navy Club (1847); Manchester Art Treasures Exhibition (1856); the National Gallery

(1866) and the Midland Hotel, St Pancras Station (1868) in all of which he was unsuccessful. He was awarded the Gold Medal of the Royal Institute of British Architects in 1856; the Order of King Leopold of the Belgians and the Order of SS. Maurice and Lazarus. His publications included *Plans, Elevations, Sections and Details of the Alhambra* (1842-46); *The Grammar of Ornament* (1856); and many smaller gift books, some of which he designed and printed himself. Jones was much involved with the setting up of the Museum of Ornamental Art, now the Victoria and Albert Museum, and the re-erection of the Crystal Palace at Sydenham, in the early 1850s. He died at his home 9, Argyll Street, London, on 19 April 1874.

LANE, Edward William (1801-1876)

Born 17 September 1801 at Hereford and educated at the Grammar Schools there and in Bath. Moved to London to learn engraving under Charles Heath to whom his elder brother Richard James was apprenticed. Became ill and having been advised to move to a warmer climate set sail for Alexandria in July 1825 arriving there some two months later. Moved to Cairo and in March 1836 set out on his first Nile voyage, making a large number of drawings of monuments particularly at Thebes where he remained for two months. On his return to Cairo commenced a detailed study of the inhabitants, their manners and customs. Made another voyage down the Nile. Early in 1828 was back in Cairo, and returned to England in the autumn of the same year. Subsequently returned to Egypt between December 1833 and August 1835 in order to continue his work in Cairo. During this time he is said to have lived 'the life of an Egyptian man of learning'. The result of his labours was the well known *Account of the Manners and Customs of the Modern Egyptians* (1836), which was followed by his translation of the *Arabian Nights Entertainments* (1838-40). Both volumes were immediately popular and ran through many editions.

In July 1842 Lane set sail for Egypt a third time, accompanied by his wife and his sister, in order to pursue his interest in the Arabic language. He remained for seven years working twelve to fourteen hours a day transcribing and translating Arabic texts, and only left Cairo once, for a period of three days to visit the pyramids. After returning to England in October 1849 he settled at Worthing, and for more than twenty-five years continued to devote himself to his lexicographic studies. The result of these labours was eventually published as the *Arabic-English Lexicon* (1863-1892, completed after his death by S. Lane Poole) which earned for him world-wide fame and many honours. Lane died on 10 August 1876.

There is a plaster seated figure of him in Arabic dress by his brother in the National Portrait Gallery, and an unpublished volume of 101 sepia drawings, including views of Cairo, in the British Museum.

LEWIS, John Frederick (1805-1876)

Born in London on 14 July 1805. His family was artistic and as a boy he studied under Edwin Landseer painting animals in particular. His first picture was apparently exhibited at the British Institution in 1820, and in the following year he also showed at the Royal Academy. Most of these early works were animal studies. In about 1825 he took up water-colours. Lewis's foreign travels commenced in 1827 when he visited Switzerland and Italy. Subsequently he travelled to Spain in 1832-4, to Paris in 1837, to Rome where he settled between 1838-40, and finally to Cairo where he lived between 1841 and 1851. During much of this time he did not exhibit in London. When he did show 'The Hareem' in 1850 it was much praised, particularly by Ruskin, who described it as 'faultlessly marvellous'. After this Lewis was hailed as a Pre-Raphaelite although he never associated with them. Elected President of the R.W.S. in 1855, but resigned to take up oil painting again. Elected an Associate of the Royal Academy in 1859 and RA in 1865. All of the Near Eastern subjects he exhibited after his return from the East were worked up in London from sketches he had made in Cairo and elsewhere. Lewis died in 1876 and his studio was sold at Christies on 4 May 1877.

LEWIS, Thomas Hayter (1818-1898)

Began his architectural career in the office of Joseph Parkinson and afterwards in that of Sir William Tite where he worked on the drawings of the Royal Exchange. During this time he won the silver medal at the Royal Academy Schools for a measured drawing of the Oxford and Cambridge Club. Entered into partnership with Thomas Finden, the brother of the engraver, in 1849, and remained with him for ten years. Subsequently continued in practice for some years before taking up a professorship at University College in 1864 where he remained until his death. He erected several large country houses in the neighbourhood of London including The Hall, Warninglid, Sussex; Staplehurst Place, Kent; Stone Lodge, Horsham; the Knowle, Brenchley; and Denham Lodge, Uxbridge. Amongst his other architectural work was a large chapel and music room added to the Infant Orphan Asylum, Wanstead, several large wharves and warehouses, and the completion of University College, London. His travels were frequent, and extended from 1841, when he visited France, Italy and Greece, until 1884. During the years from 1859-69 he made several trips to Algeria. He was Honorary Secretary of the Royal Institute of British Architects with Charles Nelson in 1859.

MOULD, Jacob Wrey (1825-1886)

Born at Chislehurst, Kent in 1825 and educated at King's College, London. Articled to Owen Jones and while working with him visited Spain to take measurements, etc. of the Alhambra. Worked on several of Jones's books including *Gray's Elegy* (1846), the *Alhambra* (1845), the *Book of Common Prayer* (1849) and the *Grammar of Ornament* (1856), and assisted with the decoration and arrangement of the Great Exhibition. During this time Directories record him as living at 12 Keppel Street, Bloomsbury. In the spring of 1853 he moved to New York where he immediately received important commissions to design All Souls Unitarian Church and the Union Club on 5th Avenue. Remained in New York for twenty years and established himself as architect, decorator, musician, song writer and translator of operas. Contemporaries described him variously as 'that strange genius', as an 'irresponsible bohemian', and as 'ugly and uncouth'. While resident in New York he also carried out various works in Central Park, including the Metropolitan Museum of Art, (1859-86); the Second Unitarian Church at Brooklyn (1857-8) and the West Presbyterian Church (1863-65). In 1875 he moved to Lima in Peru and remained there for five years before returning to New York. In 1857 he was one of the founder members of American Institute of Architects.

MURPHY, James Cavanah (1760-1814)

Born at Blackrock near Cork in 1760. Took up bricklaying but subsequently moved to Dublin to study drawing and architecture. His name appears in a list of the pupils of the drawing school of the Dublin Society about 1775 as working in miniature, chalk and crayons. In 1786 he was one of the seven architects consulted about additions to the Irish House of Commons, and to him and another was entrusted the execution of James Gandon's design. Made two visits to Spain and Portugal between 1788 and 1809. He died in London on 12 September 1814. He was unmarried, and his estate of £5,000 was administered by his sister Hannah, the wife of Bernard McNamara.

A drawing by Murphy for the completion of the Monument of King Emmanual is in the British Museum; a volume of studies and copies of Murphy's letters is in the Society of Antiquaries; and a sketch and notebook of 1790, and 46 drawings of carved panels from a Spanish Renaissance building are in the Royal Institute of British Architects.

ROBERTS, David (1796-1864)

Born at Stockbridge, near Edinburgh, the son of a shoemaker. Apprenticed for seven years to a local house painter and during this time made drawings of architectural monuments. When aged 21 he became scene painter with a circus which travelled around in the north of England. Subsequently returned to Scotland to paint scenery for theatres in Glasgow and Edinburgh, before in 1822 moving to London where he painted scenery at Drury Lane. When the Society of British Artists was formed in the following year he became its Vice President, and President in 1830. During this period he gradually gave up scene painting to concentrate on architectural subjects. In 1831 he travelled to France, the first of several tours abroad. Between 1832-3 he travelled in Italy. As a result of these tours he published *Picturesque Sketches in Spain during the Years 1832 and 1833* and *Views in the Holy Land, Syria Idumea, Arabia, Egypt and Nubia* (1842-49) in six large folio volumes. He died on 25 November 1864 in Berners Street, London and is buried at Norwood Cemetery.

SCOLES, Joseph John (1798-1863)

Born in London on 27 June 1798, the son of a joiner. His parents were Roman Catholics and he was educated at the Roman Catholic school at Baddesley Green. Apprenticed for seven years from 1812 to Joseph Ireland, the leading Roman Catholic architect of the day. In 1822 he made a tour of Italy, Greece, Egypt and Syria, returning in 1826 when he resumed architectural practice. In 1828 he undertook part of the Regent's Park Terraces with John Nash. In 1830 he erected a suspension bridge over the River Bure at Great Yarmouth which collapsed as a result of faulty workmanship some fifteen years later. It was as a designer of churches, nearly all Roman Catholic, that he was best known. These included the Brompton Oratory, of which only the residential block still remains, and the Church of the Immaculate Conception, Grosvenor Square, his most famous work.

Scoles was one of the original members of the Institute of British Architects; acted as Honorary Secretary from 1846-56, and was Vice-President 1857-8. He died at his residence Crofton Lodge, Hammersmith on 29 December 1863.

SIMPSON, William (1823-1899)

Born in Glasgow and intended to become an engineer but by 1839 was apprenticed to a local firm of lithographers. In 1851 he came to London and was employed by various architects and lithographers including Owen Jones, and Day and Son. When the Crimean War broke out he was sent by Colnaghis to make documentary drawings which were published as *The Seat of the War in the East* (1855) and established Simpson's reputation. From 1859-62 he travelled in India and Tibet making further sets of drawings. In 1866 he joined the staff of the *Illustrated London News* and covered various events including the marriage of Alexander III in St Petersburg; the Franco-German War; and the Afghan Expedition in 1878-9. He subsequently returned to Afghanistan in 1884, his last long journey. He exhibited at various galleries in the last twenty years of his life. His other major published works were Brackenbury's *Campaign in the Crimea*

(1855), and his own *India Ancient and Modern* (1867).

TEXIER, Charles Felix Marie (1802-1871)

Born Versailles 29 August 1802, the son of an architect. Became a pupil of Fr. Debret and in 1825 was appointed 'Inspecteur des Travaux' in Paris. In 1826 he was entrusted with the restoration of the ancient triumphal arch at Rheims, and in 1827 the Minister of the Interior employed him to examine the harbours of Fréjus in the South of France, to ascertain whether the level of the Mediterranean was the same then as it had been in ancient times. It was the success of this undertaking, for which Texier was awarded the first gold medals for the study of archaeology in 1831 and 1832, that persuaded the French government to employ him to make the journeys to the Middle East detailed under nos. 40-41 in the catalogue. In June 1837, between his third and fourth visits to the Near East, he was awarded the Légion d'Honneur.

After returning from his fourth journey, Texier was sent by the government in 1842 to excavate the site of the Temple of Diana Leucophryne, and to transport the sculptures he found to Paris. The friezes of the temple are now in the Louvre. In 1845 he was appointed Inspector General of Works in Algeria by Marshal Soult, and made his residence there until 1859, visiting all the settlements and making numerous drawings of Roman and other antiquities. For the last three or four years of his life his health was poor and he died at Vichy on 1 July 1871.

VULLIAMY, Lewis (1791-1871)

Born on 15 March 1791, the son of Benjamin Vulliamy, the well known clockmaker. He was articled to Sir Robert Smirke, and attended classes at the Royal Academy in 1809, winning medals in 1810 and 1813. In 1818 he was awarded the Academy's travelling studentship and made an extended Grand Tour lasting for four years. On his return he began to exhibit at the Royal Academy, and set up his architectural practice. In London he designed the Law Institution in Chancery Lane, re-fronted the Royal Institution in Albermarle Street with an impressive range of Corinthian columns, and provided 'urbane elevations for speculative builders in Bloomsbury'. Perhaps his best known works are Dorchester House, the large mansion he designed for R.S. Holford in Park Lane, for which Alfred Stevens provided the interiors (now demolished), and Westonbirt House in Gloucestershire, for the same client. His obituaries note that he was a thoroughly professional architect who prided himself on the accuracy of his estimates and on a 'remarkable ingenuity both mechanical and mental'. A commentator in the *Builder*, however, noted that he was 'also well known to be peculiar in his notions, and many odd anecdotes are related of him.' Vulliamy married Elizabeth Papendiek, the only daughter of the Revd Frederick

Papendiek, and had four sons with all of whom he quarrelled. He died at his residence on Clapham Common on 4 January 1871.

WARREN, Albert Henry (1830-1911)

Born on 5 May 1830 the eldest son of Henry Warren, (see following entry). Articled to Owen Jones and worked with him on the decoration and internal arrangement of the Great Exhibition (his entry in *Who Was Who* also states that he was 'engaged in the construction' of the building) and on preparing the plates for several of Jones's books including the *Grammar of Ornament* (1856), for which he also helped gather the material, and the *Alhambra* (1842-46). He also did the drawings for the St. James's Hall, Piccadilly, London (1856), designed by Jones. Assisted his father in painting panoramas of the Nile and the Holy Land, and helped his uncle John Martin with the designs for the Thames Embankment. He was at one time Professor of Landscape at Queen's College, London; and gave lessons for four years to Princess Alice and Princess Helena in the art of illuminating. He exhibited one picture at the Royal Academy, and four at the Royal Society of British Artists. His hobby was volunteering and he was in the Artists' Rifles, 20th Middlesex, for twenty-five years. He was a pensioner of the Royal Academy and received grants from the Royal Bounty Fund. His publications included *A Guide to Beginners in the Art of Illumination* (1860); *Drawing Examples for Technical and Art Students* (1882); and a *Garden Painting Book* (1889). He married Augusta, the only daughter of Thomas Tyreman and died on 2 March 1911.

WARREN, Henry (1794-1879)

Born in London in 1794. Studied sculpture under Nollekens with John Gibson and Joseph Bonomi, and entered the Royal Academy Schools. He soon determined to abandon sculpture and take up oil painting, and subsequently exhibited several works in that medium at the Royal Academy. When the New Society of Painters in Water-Colours was established in 1835 he joined it and became President in 1839, a position he held until 1873, when failing health and imperfect eyesight obliged him to resign. From the time that he joined the New Society until his death he almost invariably worked in water-colours exhibiting no less than 244 at the annual exhibitions. Warren's principal works were of Arabian subjects though he apparently never visited the East. He wrote several books on subjects connected with painting including *Hints upon Tints, with Strokes upon Copper and Canvass* (1833); *Painting in Water-Colours* (1856); *A Text Book of Art Studies* (1870); and *A Treatise on Figure Drawing* (1871). He also illustrated many books by other authors.

Warren was knighted by Leopold, King of the Belgians, in recognition of his talents as an artist, and was an Honorary member of the Société Belge des Aquarellistes, and of the Pennsylvania Academy of Arts. He was several times appointed a Commissioner of Fine Arts for International Exhibitions. He had two sons Albert H. and Edmund J. both of whom became artists. He died at 8 Cornwall Terrace, Wimbledon, on 18 December 1879.

WILD, James William (1814-1892)

Born on 9 March 1814 the son of Charles Wild, the author of several popular volumes on cathedrals. Served his architectural apprenticeship with George Basevi, and studied architecture at the Royal Academy. After completing his training, Basevi entrusted Wild with the design of several small gothic churches including All Saints, Botley (1836) and St Saviours, Southampton (from 1839). These were followed in 1840 by his most famous church, Christ Church at Streatham. In 1842 he joined the great German expedition to Egypt led by Lepsius, with Joseph Bonomi, and after returning to England in 1848, was appointed 'Referee' concerning Arabian Art at the South Kensington Museum.

Wild's other architectural work included the influential St. Martin's Schools, Endell Street, London (1849, now demolished); the tower at Grimsby docks (1849); the British legation at Teheran; St. Mark's Church, Alexandria; and various works for the Department of Science and Art including the cast courts at the South Kensington Museum, and the Bethnal Green Museum. In 1878 Wild was appointed Curator of Sir John Soane's Museum in succession to Joseph Bonomi. He died in November 1892.

WYATT, Sir Matthew Digby (1820-1877)

Born at Rowde, near Devizes in 1820, the younger brother of T.H. Wyatt, the architect, to whom he was articled. Travelled on the continent 1844-46. In 1849 he reported to the Society of Arts on an industrial exhibition held in Paris, and in 1851 was appointed Secretary to the Executive Committee for the Great Exhibition. In 1855 he became Surveyor to the East India Company. Wyatt's work included the Byzantine, English Gothic, Italian, and Renaissance Courts at the Crystal Palace at Sydenham, (1854); Paddington Station, London (1854-5 in association with I.K. Brunel); chapel at Warley Barracks, Essex (1857); Royal Engineers' Crimean War Memorial, Chatham (1861); fernery in the gardens of Ashridge House, Herts. (1864); Addenbroke's Hospital, Cambridge (1864-5); Possingworth Manor, Sussex (1866); Government Offices, Whitehall, London (1867 with Sir G.G. Scott); and Oldlands, Herron's Ghyll, Sussex (1869). He was Honorary Secretary of the Royal Institute of British Architects, 1855-9; Vice-President and received the Gold Medal 1866. Awarded the Telford Medal of the Institute of Civil Engineers, and various foreign honours. First Slade Professor of Fine Arts, Cambridge. President of the Graphic Society. His many published works included *Specimens of the Geometrical Mosaics of the Middle Ages* (1848); *The Industrial Arts of the Nineteenth Century* (1851-3); *Metalwork and its Artistic Design* (1852); *Illuminated Manuscripts as Illustrative of the Arts of Design* (1860); *The History of the Manufacture of Clocks* (1868) and *An Architect's Note Book in Spain* (1872). He died in 1877 and is buried at Usk, Monmouthshire.

ZANTH, Karl Ludwig Wilhelm von (1796-1857)

Born in 1796 in Breslau, the son of an eminent medical man who was chief physician to Jerome Buonaparte during his residence at Cassel. Educated in Cassel and under Charles Percier in Paris. Moved to Stuttgart where his widowed mother lived, and became a pupil of Fischer, professor of the Polytechnic there. In 1819 returned to Paris as the pupil, and later the assistant of Jacob Ignaz Hittorff. In 1823 accompanied Hittorff to Sicily where they made measured drawings of classical and post classical buildings subsequently published in two volumes *L'Architecture antique de la Sicile*, Paris 1826-35. In 1830 Zanth left Paris and returned to Stuttgart where he built 'many charming town and country houses, perfectly adapted to the convenience of the occupants, elegant in detail, picturesque in their masses', and designed a grand opera house, art school and museum which were not carried out. These works came under the notice of King Wilhelm I of Württemberg who immediately appointed him as his architect. Zanth designed the Königsbau for the King, which was built after Zanth's death by his pupil C.F. Leins, a protestant church to be attached to the Royal Palace, and the Villa Wilhelma, the building which occupied him for the rest of his life. While working on the Villa he designed a large village for a wealthy landowner in Hungary 'with houses and farms of different sizes, a church, and other public buildings in connection with the restored castle of the Lord. These designs are of the greatest interest; for he scrupulously studied to make them conform to the materials at command ... and gave them a national character, elevated by elegant and appropriate combinations and proportions, without departing from simplicity and utility.'

In 1856 Zanth visited Italy with Hittorff in an attempt to revive his failing health, but 'his residence of some months in Rome was one of suffering and discomfort'. He died on 7 October 1857 shortly after his return, and while on his deathbed received the 'Commander of the Order of Stanislaus' from the Emperor of Russia who awarded it to him personally having been enchanted by the Villa Wilhelma. He had previously received decorations from the Pope, the Great Duke of Baden, and the Duchess Regent of Parma.

There are drawings by Zanth in the Stadtbibliothek and Wallraf-Richartz Museum, Cologne, and the Ecole des Beaux Arts, Paris.

INDEX

Figure 8